THE RAILROADERS

THE OLD WEST

THE RAILROADERS

By the Editors of

TIME-LIFE BOOKS

with text by

Keith Wheeler

TIME-LIFE BOOKS, NEW YORK

THE OLD WEST

EDITORIAL STAFF FOR "THE RAILROADERS"
Editor: Ezra Bowen
Picture Editor: Grace Brynolson
Text Editor: William Frankel
Designer: Herbert H. Quarmby
Staff Writers: Erik Amfitheatrof, Michael Drons,
Philip Payne, Suzanne Seixas, Bryce Walker, Peter Wood
Chief Researcher: Joan Mebane
Researchers: Monica Borrowman, Loretta Britten,
Malabar Brodeur, Catherine Ireys, Peggy S. Jackson,
Mary Leverty, Mary Kay Moran, Ann Morrison,
Gail Nussbaum, Wendy Reider, Jane Sugden,
John C. Weiser
Design Assistant: Anne B. Landry

EDITORIAL PRODUCTION
Production Editor: Douglas B. Graham
Assistant Production Editors: Gennaro C. Esposito,
Feliciano Madrid
Quality Director: Robert L. Young
Assistant Quality Director: James J. Cox
Associate: Serafino J. Cambareri
Copy Staff: Eleanore W. Karsten (chief),
Barbara H. Fuller, Ricki Tarlow, Florence Keith,
Pearl Sverdlin
Picture Department: Dolores A. Littles,
Barbara S. Simon
Traffic: Carmen McLellan

THE AUTHOR: Keith Wheeler grew up on the North Dakota prairie about 200 yards from the tracks of the Minneapolis, St. Paul & Sault Ste. Marie Railroad. After 15 years as a reporter, columnist and foreign correspondent for newspapers in the West and Middle West, he joined the staff of LIFE magazine in 1951 as a writer. Now a freelance living in New York, he has published five novels and two nonfiction volumes based on his experiences as a war correspondent in the Pacific Theater during World War II campaigns.

THE COVER: With the advent of the transcontinental railroad in 1869, the wilderness of the American West succumbed to a glamorous new machine — a huffing behemoth like the one in the cover lithograph by Currier & Ives, which shows a Central Pacific locomotive highballing through the Sierra Nevada in California. But the machine was run by men. Most of them were obscure yet intensely proud individuals very much like those seen in the frontispiece photograph — Chicago, Burlington & Northern maintenance workers standing on a handcar. Their picture was taken in 1888 by an unknown photographer.

Valuable assistance was provided by the following departments and individuals of Time Inc.: Editorial Production, Norman Airey; Library, Benjamin Lightman; Picture Collection, Doris O'Neil; Photographic Laboratory, George Karas; TIME-LIFE News Service, Murray J. Gart; Correspondents Jane Estes (Seattle), Martha Green (San Francisco), Pat Tucker (Washington), Leslie Ward (Los Angeles), Sue Wymelenberg (Boston).

TIME
LIFE
BOOKS
®

CONTENTS

1|A work of visionaries -- or of fools?

As late as the 1850s the notion that a Bostonian could soon buy a railroad ticket to California and be there within a week seemed as remote as the fantasies of Jules Verne. There was even good cause to doubt whether railroad technology could ever cope with the physical challenge of the American West *(following pages)*. Besides the country's dizzying breadth, there was the killing desert, not to mention Indians who had already taken their toll of advance survey parties. Then there were formidable mountain ranges to cross, with snow-clogged passes and steep river canyons. "A railroad to the Pacific?" scoffed a prominent government official in 1862. "I would not buy a ticket on it for my grandchildren." Railroads, as he and everyone else knew, were intended primarily to connect thriving population centers like New York and Philadelphia, with plenty of people and freight to be picked up and delivered at many points along the route. But the West, from Missouri to California, was 2,000 miles of sparsely populated wilderness.

What the skeptics overlooked—and a handful of visionaries and vigorous entrepreneurs did not—was that with the help of federal loans and land grants the job could be done in short order. Settlement, like water flowing into an irrigation ditch, would surely follow. And that is exactly what happened.

Outside Omaha, in 1866, the first miles of Union Pacific roadbed, minus rails, point west across an empty prairie.

7

A Denver & Rio Grande train, with two engines pulling, inches up the side of a granite gorge in the heart of the Rockies. Carving the right of way through country like this was heartbreakingly slow, requiring tons of blasting powder and often measuring no more than a few feet per day.

A Central Pacific construction train rolls along new track, headed east across the alkali flats of the Humboldt Desert, in 1868. After the terrible grades of the Sierra, work crews blessed the flatland — until they were plagued by the heat and the absence of appreciable amounts of water.

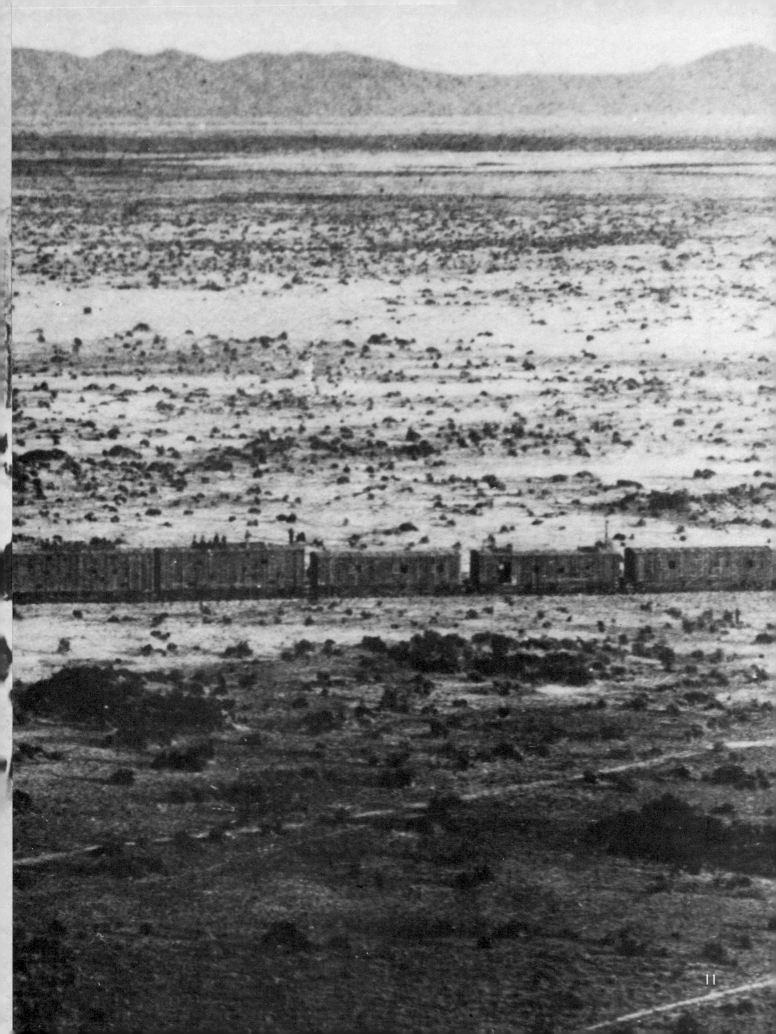

Three engines with tenders and two cabooses test the strength of an iron-trussed span at Weber Canyon, Utah, in 1869. An earlier bridge, hastily built of cottonwood timbers by Union Pacific construction crews during their race west, had been swept away by the first spring floods.

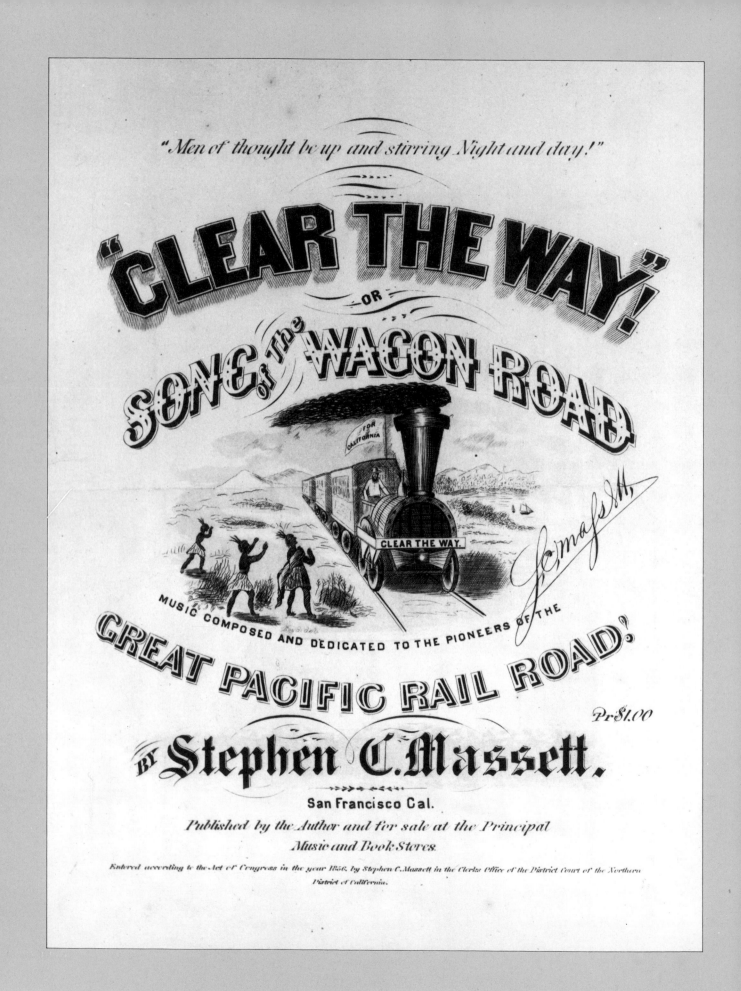

A scheme "to annihilate magnificent distances"

No humor was intended in the railroad's choice of a name. The Pacific Railroad of Missouri, the directors called it. And their single locomotive, a hissing, high-wheeled contraption with a blunderbuss smokestack, bore the same hopeful name—the *Pacific*. For the moment, to be sure, the only tangible sign of a link between Missouri and the Pacific was a five-mile stretch of track running westward from St. Louis. But with all the pride (and an encouraging measure of the wealth) of that thriving river port solidly behind them, the P.R.R.M.'s promoters were not ashamed to be labeled optimists and boosters. No man ever lost money betting on the future of Missouri, sir. And who was to say that the engines and the trains the new railroad expected to acquire would not some day reach the Pacific and live up to the name?

On this historic afternoon, however, it was quite enough to stoke up the *Pacific*'s wood-fired boiler and, with two cars of local politicians, investors, wives and well-scrubbed children in tow, go chugging down the P.R.R.M.'s iron rails to the town of Cheltenham, just outside of St. Louis. That would suffice to establish December 9, 1852, as the day passengers first rode a train west of the Mississippi River.

In Cheltenham the travelers repaired to a feast at the mansion of Mr. Hawley, one of the richest men in town. As reported by the *Missouri Republican,* a round of speeches followed, by P.R.R.M. president Thomas Allen, by the Mayor of St. Louis and by sundry lesser functionaries. According to the *Republican,* Mr. O'Sullivan, the chief construction engineer of the road, "was most flatteringly toasted by the company. The health of Mr. Williams, who ran the first locomotive, was received with cheers." By the time the oratory was over, none present could doubt that 10,000 hands on 10,000 throttles would follow Mr. Williams, transforming St. Louis into the hub of a continent tied together by iron rails.

For the utmost in pomp and ceremony, the occasion lacked only one man's voice. Missing from the speaker's rostrum was the distinguished Congressman from Missouri, the ever-expansive expansionist Thomas Hart Benton, who had business that day in the halls of Congress. For more than eight years Benton had been extolling a transcontinental railroad as a great instrument of prosperity—with St. Louis, of course, as the natural terminus. And his determined vision of a Western railroad inspired some of his finest oratory. In one of many speeches to the Senate, Benton said of the railroad that "emigrants would flock upon it as pigeons to their roosts, tear open the bosom of the virgin soil, and spring into existence the long line of farms and houses, of towns and villages, of orchards, fields, and gardens, of churches and schoolhouses, of noisy shops, clattering mills and thundering forges, and all that civilization affords to enliven the wild domain from the Mississippi to the Pacific." And that was only the half of it. Benton also saw a transcontinental railroad as the shortest route between Europe and the fabulous riches of the Orient, a kind of caravan road on rails that would provide an indispensable advantage to American merchants plying the China trade.

But even Benton was not such a wild visionary as to imagine the gaudy spectacle that would actually be played out in the West. Within the span of a single generation Congress and state governments would grant more than 116 million acres to Western railroads, and would advance $64 million in bonds to these

On this song cover even the Indians welcome the arrival of the transcontinental train. Composed by a boosterish San Franciscan, the tune was published in 1856, at the peak of the early railroad fever.

THE GREAT DEBATE over the question of a transcontinental railroad spanned three decades, flared up in the high chambers of Washington and gradually enveloped the whole nation. Some leaders were not convinced that there should even be such a railroad; for others the critical issue was precisely where it would go.

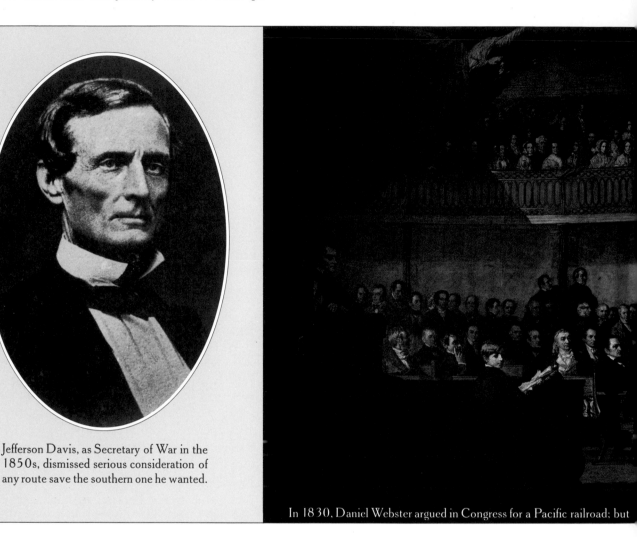

Jefferson Davis, as Secretary of War in the 1850s, dismissed serious consideration of any route save the southern one he wanted.

In 1830, Daniel Webster argued in Congress for a Pacific railroad; but

roads. Fertilized by such financing, trans-Mississippi track mileage would leap upward from those five miles in 1852 to more than 72,000 miles in 1890. And by 1893 there would be not one road but five Pacific railroads with dozens of feeder lines crosshatching the land between.

Within that time these roads would give life to the country's hopes for its frontier. They would stitch together all the emptiness of the West. And long before the 19th Century was out, passenger trains with liquor and pianos aboard would rumble out of New York in the full expectation that they would arrive in San Francisco a mere 84 hours later. At the same time the rail lines would become a critical framework for the greatest industrial combine in world history, an edifice of money, real estate, technology and political leverage so pow-

erful that the very era would afterward be known as the Railroad Period.

And if the changes to come would be great and gaudy, the cast of characters would be equally so. There would be the makers: the bold surveyors, the brawling Irish construction workers and their sober Chinese counterparts, the daring and ingenious corporate promoters, the proud engineers and the sooty-faced firemen. And there would be the takers: those same corporate promoters, men in muttonchop whiskers and waistcoats, who would practice high finance and low politics and would one day stand revealed as some of the 19th Century's most distinguished scoundrels.

Above all there was the sheer physical momentum of the project. Once started, construction crews spanning the continent would brush aside distance and des-

eight years later Webster said the West was only a worthless void.

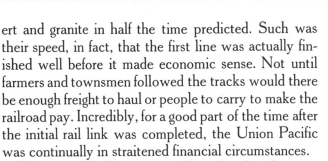

President Abraham Lincoln, in the midst of the Civil War, finally ended the debate by signing the Pacific Railroad Act of 1862.

ert and granite in half the time predicted. Such was their speed, in fact, that the first line was actually finished well before it made economic sense. Not until farmers and townsmen followed the tracks would there be enough freight to haul or people to carry to make the railroad pay. Incredibly, for a good part of the time after the initial rail link was completed, the Union Pacific was continually in straitened financial circumstances.

Miners and cattlemen were there already, of course, to welcome the road—and they could hardly suppress their astonishment at the sight of conductors in tailored coats and brass buttons consulting gold watches marked in hours, minutes and seconds in a region that still measured its time by seasons. In retrospect, this course of events may have been inevitable. But despite their brave words the celebrants at Cheltenham in 1852 could not

have realized what the railroads would accomplish.

Against their optimism was pitted the dim view of Western development put forth by such contemporary luminaries as the great Daniel Webster. Though Webster had once made a congenial wave in the direction of a Pacific railroad, by 1845 he had gone completely sour on the West. "What do we want with this region of savages and wild beasts, of deserts, of shifting sands and whirlwinds of dust, of cactus and prairie dogs?" the Senator from Massachusetts had demanded of his colleagues. "To what use could we ever put those endless mountain ranges? . . . What could we do with the western coast line three thousand miles away, rock-bound, cheerless and uninviting?"

No one was listening. For years men had captured the American imagination by insisting that the West was worth winning, and for at least two decades other men had been saying that the way to win it was to build a railroad there.

One of the earliest concrete proposals had come from Dr. Hartwell Carver of Rochester, New York. In 1832 he had published a series of articles in the *New York Courier & Enquirer* proposing a transcontinental railroad line. Later he suggested that the government reserve eight million acres of federally owned land for a railroad running from Lake Michigan to Oregon Country. He even went so far as to present Congress with a memorandum in which he envisioned cross-country luxury trains with cars 100 feet long that contained dining rooms and sleeping berths. The completed project, Carver declared in a flight of eloquence, would "bring about a kind of earthly millennium, and be the means of uniting the whole world in one great church, a part of whose worship will be to praise God and bless the Oregon Railroad."

The doctor was clearly ahead of his time. In the 1830s the 136-mile railroad from Charleston to Hamburg, South Carolina, was the longest in the world. Other lines were beginning to spring up across the Eastern U.S. and the South, but most of them were extinguished in the financial panic of 1837. Though a few of the stronger lines managed to survive, the shaky new science of steam locomotion still appeared so dubious that in 1839 a railroad in Kentucky decided to forget any plans for pulling cars with a steam engine and made do with horses.

To project such tenuous beginnings across the unmapped reaches of the West required a leap of imagination too great for most practical men. The distance from the Missouri to the Pacific was some 1,600 miles. Within that expanse rose not one but two mountain chains, the Rocky Mountains and the Sierra Nevada; in both ranges peaks soared above 14,000 feet, and winter snows piled up in the passes to depths of 40 feet and more. Upon such a raw wilderness, it seemed impossible that man could impose 1,600 miles of cuts and fills, of tunnels and bridges, of freightyards and roundhouses and elegant passenger depots. Perhaps even more formidable, between the mountains lay the arid wasteland of the Great Basin, hundreds of miles wide, where water for men and locomotive boilers was scarce and corrosively alkaline, and wood for fireboxes

and for railroad ties was almost as rare as a rainy day.

There was a psychological barrier, too. In an era when many Americans had never traveled more than a good day's walk from their birthplace, the Western country that the railroad people were proposing to cross was still very much terra incognita, downright dangerous and just plain too big. The overland horse trail to California had first been completed by mountain man Joe Walker as late as 1833. Since then, pioneers who dared make the journey had taken four to six months to creep across the inhospitable and often hostile land from the Missouri River to California. Many who started never made it.

Even some of those intrepid Americans who had managed to reach the West Coast tended to be dubious about the proposed railroad; and they spoke with the authority of pioneers who knew the rigors and perils of the journey. "We will not consent to view this 'stupendous project' practicable for a number of years to come," wrote the editor of *The California Star.* "The depredatory acts of intractable Indians, directly through whose country the route lies, is one of a series of obstacles to the actual execution of the work." So the idea of a transcontinental railroad remained a kind of heroic mirage until 1844, when a most unusual and persuasive man arrived home from China.

Asa Whitney, a New York City merchant, had grown rich trading in the Orient. And he, like Benton, was certain that a large part of his country's commercial future lay across the Pacific, if only the transcontinental railroad could be completed. And Whitney, taking over where the more modest Carver left off, was ready to commit his fortune, his time and his prodigious energy to the road.

Whitney proposed to Congress that the government sell him 77,952,000 acres for 16 cents apiece —whereupon, without further fuss and with no other financing, he would put his plan in operation. Under this scheme, Whitney proposed that he should sell some parcels of his land to settlers, start a railroad out of the profits, sell more land, build more road and go inching across the continent in perfect solvency. Farmer and trainman would thus claim and tame a 60-mile-wide swath of virgin territory from Lake Michigan to the mouth of the Columbia River, crossing the Rockies where the mountain man's trail did, at South Pass. ◉

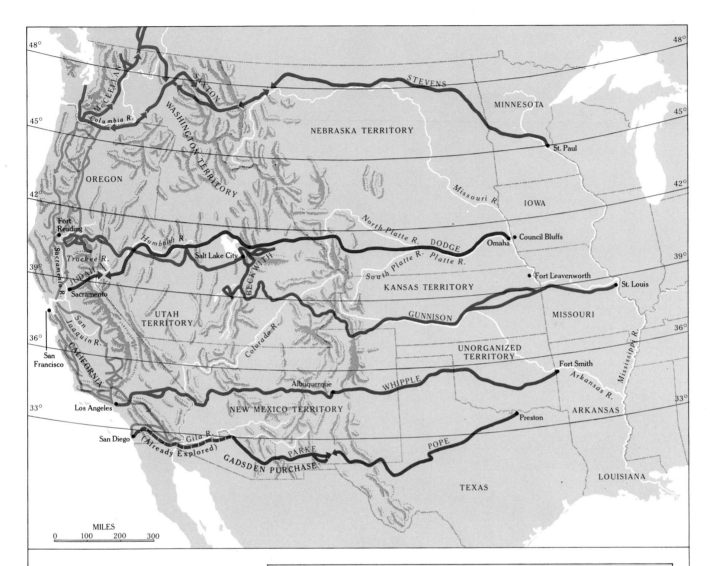

RAILROADS EAST AND SURVEYS WEST

Five major surveys explored possible routes for completion of the first transcontinental railroad. Four of the routes (shown above in blue, with the names of their principal surveyors) were finished in the 1850s by the U.S. government, which also made connecting surveys in Oregon and California (green). But the fifth survey (red) determined the railroad's final course. Theodore Judah and Grenville Dodge mapped the path for the iron rails that would bind the Pacific Coast to the network of more than 30,000 miles of track existing in the Eastern United States by 1860 (right).

Fighting the swollen Hell Gate River in Montana Territory, three surveyors along the 47th parallel wrestle their gear off a sinking raft.

Whitney, a guilelessly messianic man, saw himself engaged in no less a crusade than completing the work of Columbus: both he and the great Italian navigator, he pointed out to any Senator or Congressman who cared to listen, proposed to take to the West in order to gain the East.

After five years of hard campaigning throughout the state capitals and a personal trek by horseback over a sizable portion of his route, Whitney had won the official endorsement of 17 state legislatures and returned to Congress riding a strong current of public approval.

One state whose support Whitney did not have, however, was Missouri. Senator Benton and his cronies in Congress had been hatching their own scheme for a Pacific railroad based on the principle of government ownership and, naturally enough, having St. Louis as its eastern terminus rather than Chicago or some other Great Lakes port. The latter objective probably concerned them most, but they used the issue of private ownership in order to attack Whitney. His plan, declared Representative J. B. Bowlin of Missouri, would put the states in a "humiliating condition, subject to the power of one man." It would, he protested, irrevocably commit "the blood and treasure of the nation —for the sole and exclusive benefit of Mr. Whitney and his assigns."

Most of this, of course, was nonsense. Whitney had demonstrated beyond any reasonable doubt that he was an honest man in an age not known for corporate scruples, and his designs for a transcontinental railroad were more altruistic than profit-motivated. Nevertheless, by the time Benton and his forces were through castigating him, Congress had been induced to table the Whitney plan without a vote (although in the discussion preceding this action, members pointed out that Whitney had proposed to overcharge himself by six cents an acre for the lands he wished to purchase).

In addition to this rebuff, Whitney found his proposal coming under heavy fire from railroad experts who deplored his ingenuous disregard for the physical realities of building railroads. In April 1851, the authoritative *American Railroad Journal* complained: "He has a hearty contempt for the whole engineering profession and loses his temper the moment one of that class talks about tunneling, bridging, excavation, etc. which are certainly great annoyances in railroad construction . . . but is never tired of enlarging upon the grandeur of his scheme."

Whitney made many attempts to reply to these critics; but it was true that he knew very little about engineering. He could not persuade the Congress to reconsider. As a last recourse he took his idea to England, suggesting that the British build across Canada. But England, too, turned him down, and Whitney at last acknowledged defeat. With what was left of his fortune, he retired to a comfortable estate outside Washington, D.C. But he had accomplished a great deal. In the course of his failure he had generated so much curiosity and excitement that the nation was substantially convinced that the Pacific railroad was no zealot's dream, but an inevitability. And indeed before Whitney died in 1872, one transcontinental railroad had been completed and three others begun.

While attacking the Whitney plan, Benton made one very positive contribution toward pushing a railroad across the West. "We must have surveys, examinations, and explorations made, and not go blindfolded, haphazard into such a scheme," he told the Senate. He thus pinpointed a basic and ruinous flaw in every other Pacific railroad project: the still-vague notion of the critical details of Western geography that prevailed 40 to 50 years after Lewis and Clark.

True, the broad dimensions of the continent were known. And what appeared to be the most sensible pathway west was by now under steady use by wagon trains of emigrants and, most recently, by forty-niners. Sticking close to rivers and generally following the easiest grades, the main emigrant trail went up the Platte valley, over the Continental Divide via South Pass and

Architect of the Pacific railroad's route across the Sierra, Theodore Judah found the mountains—and the apathy of Congress —easier to conquer than the massive greed of the directors of his own Central Pacific.

At Daniel Strong's drugstore in Dutch Flat, California, the Central Pacific was born. Here in 1860 Strong told Theodore Judah of his route over the Sierra; and here, too, Judah drew up plans for his railroad. Fame had not changed it much when it was photographed several years later.

then across the Great Basin to Oregon or California. This general route might well accommodate a railroad.

But without careful surveys there was no guarantee that trains could follow where families had gone on foot or in wagons. For railroads required grades no steeper than 116 feet to the mile, a rise hardly perceptible to the human eye, and curves with a minimum 300-foot radius to keep a locomotive from jumping the track. Even if the emigrant route—or the Santa Fe Trail to the south—met these stiff criteria, no one could say for sure that a dozen equally feasible and even shorter routes did not exist somewhere out there.

With his politician's keenness for exploiting a weakness, Benton began preparing for a survey. Naturally, its basic line would start west from St. Louis. Just as naturally, the Senator had little trouble persuading wealthy friends in St. Louis to pay for the surveying expedition. And who better to lead it than Benton's own illustrious son-in-law, John C. Frémont, the man called Pathfinder for his many odysseys across the West? Accordingly, in October 1848, Frémont set out from Westport, Missouri, with a party of 35 to explore a route that Benton had dubbed the Buffalo Trail, implying a sort of sanction by the continent's most conspicuous migratory beast. In fact, it was almost a direct transit along the 38th parallel—St. Louis to San Francisco—and deserts or mountains be damned.

Besides being greatly celebrated as an explorer, soldier, promoter and budding politician, Frémont had actually worked as a railroad surveyor for the Army Topographical Corps in the mid-1830s, when he helped run the line for a railroad between Charleston and Cincinnati. This experience gave some validity to Frémont's boast that he was leading the first really expert railroad reconnaissance for a route to the Western ocean. Less valid was Frémont's notion that he could locate a clear pass over the Continental Divide in the wild, tumbling Sangre de Cristo range of the southern Rockies, at roughly the agreed-upon 38th parallel —some 300 miles below the Emigrant Trail through South Pass. From the divide, he intended to surmount the even more formidable San Juan Mountains, then cross the Great Basin and enter California by rejoining the Emigrant Trail over the Sierra.

Despite the unpromising terrain, Frémont might in fact have found some sort of feasible line had he not been fatally inspired to attempt the crossing in the dead of winter—the better to show off the Buffalo Trail's advantages as an all-weather railroad route. When his party became trapped in a mid-December snowstorm 12,000 feet up in the Rocky Mountains, the Pathfinder's mission turned into a horrifying debacle in which 10 of his men either froze or starved to death. Only through a lucky meeting with a band of friendly Ute Indians after he had abandoned the main body of his men was the Pathfinder himself rescued from a month-long ordeal for survival. "The result was entirely satisfactory," he declared with the aid of hindsight. "It convinced me that neither the snow of winter nor the mountain ranges were obstacles in the way of a road."

Armed with this good news—but still lacking firm data—Benton offered in the Senate a railroad scheme based, he said, on his son-in-law's discoveries. The Benton plan called for setting aside a 100-mile-wide strip of land straddling the 38th parallel for the construction of a "central national highway" to be built, owned and operated by the government. As with most Benton proposals, the new plan was persuasive, at least superficially. Yet he could offer no precise measurements of possible grades and curves. The fact remained that from the standpoint of railroad engineering neither Benton nor the backers of a half dozen competitive schemes actually knew what they were talking about.

That did not stop any of them from talking. The U.S. Army, which operated its own corps of Western explorers, had a plan for a transcontinental road down south along the 32nd parallel, where the troops were having the devil's own time keeping the newly won Mexican border sealed against Apache and Comanche raiders. The military also had some worries about how well California could be defended, now that it was part of the Union but still a good month's march from Texas. Though no measurements of grades and curves had been made on the Army's route either, the military men claimed that the Southern Trail would not only aid in the defense of Texas, New Mexico Territory and California but that it would also prove the shortest and least expensive from a commercial point of view. "The consequences of such a road are immense," declared Colonel John J. Abert, head of the Corps of Topographical Engineers, striking the gong not only for the Army's proposed Southern Trail but for the whole con-

cept of a Pacific railroad. "They probably involve the integrity of the Union. Unless some easy, cheap, and rapid means of communicating with these distant provinces be accomplished, there is danger, great danger, that they will not constitute parts of our Union."

Meanwhile, in a seemingly unrelated effort to help some of the shorter Eastern lines to expand, lobbyists had begun pressing for government grants of land to these roads. The principle fascinated transcontinental railroad backers. Anyone could plainly see how the benefits of this concept might be applied to help finance a Pacific railroad company.

Land, after all, was something the U.S. government owned in almost measureless quantity. It was suggested that the government might give some of it to the railroads in an intermittent sequence of sections lying alternately north and south of the proposed right of way. The government would thus be providing a commodity that the roads could sell to pay for construction, while at the same time increasing the value of the sections that it reserved for itself. Everyone would prosper. So persuasive was this logic that in 1850 President Millard Fillmore signed the first railroad land-grant act, giving 2.6 million acres to the Illinois Central and a similar acreage to a road out of Mobile, Alabama. This principle of federal patronage was recognized immediately as the kind of snowball that starts an avalanche. Between 1850 and 1860 about 20 million acres of public lands were granted to the railroads.

With this happy turn of events, a number of businessmen throughout the country hastened to line up with the President and the Army in urging the benefits of building railroads—to almost anywhere. Said one Missouri executive to an approving assemblage: "A railroad, fellow citizens, is a machine, and one of the most beautiful and perfect of labor-saving machines. It well suits the energy of the American people. They love to go ahead fast, and to go with power. They love to annihilate the magnificent distances."

In the Middle West as well as the East, distance was already being annihilated, thanks not only to the land grants but also to some giant steps that had been made in the improvement of locomotive design (*pages 38-40*). By May 1852 the first passenger train from the East had arrived in Chicago. And not a few trans-Mississippians could envision a time when railroads

The formidable, rocky wilderness of Judah's route over the Sierra Nevada from Dutch Flat to Nevada gave way to a profitable wagon road—which in turn bacame the basic line for the Central Pacific tracks.

would crosshatch the plains of Iowa, Missouri, the Kansas Territory and points west, just as the Eastern roads were now serving Pennsylvania, Ohio and Illinois.

Of course each businessman, together with his political friends, saw his own hometown as a rail hub. And with the prospect of a transcontinental line so clearly in view, each hoped his town would be the funnel through which Western commerce would pour. It was in this boosterish context that the directors of the Pacific Railroad of Missouri took such robust satisfaction in their history-making five-mile train ride from St. Louis to Cheltenham. For while that first little pair of iron rails west of the Mississippi may not have greatly resembled Senator Benton's 100-mile-wide highway, it was certainly an excellent way of informing Vicksburg and Cairo and such upstart towns as Memphis that the city of St. Louis meant to live up to its long reputation as the shoving-off place for the conquest of the West.

With all these interests jostling for favor in the location of the Pacific railroad, in March of 1853 Congress finally did the sensible thing. The lawmakers sent an appropriation of $150,000 to Secretary of War Jefferson Davis, instructing him to survey within 10 months the principal routes to the Pacific (page 21) and thereby determine which was the most "practicable and economical."

Davis at that moment had two perspectives on the West. As Secretary of War, he clearly understood what Colonel Abert and others had been saying about the military importance of a railroad. But as a wealthy Mississippi planter, and a thoughtful and influential leader of the South, he also foresaw what importance the choice of a route could have in the mounting battle over slavery and states' rights. A railroad leading west from Texas would link California to the interests and the economy of the South. A northern or central road would just as certainly exclude the South from the fruits of Western commerce, and permanently tip the balance of power to an industrial combine of Northern and Western states. The obvious compromise, to build two railroads, one north and one south, was deemed out of the question because of the expense.

Well aware of the North's political strength in Washington (both President Pierce and the Senate majority were Northern), the Secretary might have been expected to bridle when Congress proposed a review of the routes. Instead, he welcomed the move as a means to achieving his end: "If the section of which I am a citizen has the best route," he would ask, "who that looks to the interest of the country has a right to deny it the road?" These Congressional surveys would give him a perfect chance to prove that the best route was the southern route.

In its instructions to Davis, Congress called for as many surveys as there were practicable routes. The Secretary interpreted "practicable" to apply to those routes having strong political backing, rather than to the ones with the soundest engineering prospects. He omitted, for instance, the Emigrant Trail, claiming it was already too well known to warrant a survey. He also excluded his own Southern Trail, presumably to show that he was playing no favorites. Actually, he seemed to be betting that the surveys would be so hastily carried out that they would prove inconclusive, thus leaving his southern route in a commanding position.

When the surveys first got under way that summer, four parties took the field. The largest was under the command of Isaac I. Stevens, the zealous young governor of the new Washington Territory. He was to march west between the 49th and the 47th parallels, from the Great Lakes to Puget Sound. This was the so-called Northern Trail, originally suggested by Whitney and now favored by the powerful Senator Stephen Douglas of Illinois. Benton's Buffalo Trail would also be explored. A third expedition backed by Representative John Smith Phelps would study the 35th Parallel Trail from Fort Smith, Arkansas, to Albuquerque and across the Mojave Desert to the Pacific near Los Angeles. The fourth would scour the San Joaquin Valley of California for passes that might connect the 35th parallel route with Davis' own favorite Southern Trail.

These pages from Judah's notebook record his pioneering survey of the route over the Sierra crest. The right-hand columns list readings from the aneroid barometer that he employed to measure changes in altitude.

Late the following fall, under pressure from skeptics who challenged the Southern Trail's apparent lack of water, timber and a suitable pass through the mountains, Davis agreed to send out two more survey parties under Lieutenants John Pope and J. G. Parke to report on that route. He also authorized two other surveys to explore connecting routes on the Pacific Coast.

The work horses of the surveys were young Army engineers, unknown at the time but many of them destined for fame in the Civil War to come: John B. Hood, George McClellan, John Pope and Philip H. Sheridan, to name a few. Each party also took a complement of civilian scientists — including at least one geologist — and an artist. Moreover, at the request of various colleges and learned societies, Davis allowed an assortment of other civilian scholars to tag along.

These formidable task forces were equipped to answer any questions Congress might have — unless Congress was impolite enough to ask for precise data on cuts, fills and curves. The 10-month deadline left no time for these. Thus, in a manner all too reminiscent of Frémont's debacle, the critical element of engineering was largely missing from the massive reports that began flooding the War Department the following year.

Nevertheless, on the first Monday in January 1854, when the 10-month deadline imposed by the Congress

The Pacific mail ship *Sonora* carried Judah to Panama in 1859 to cross the Isthmus on his second trip east to lobby for the railroad. A similar voyage four years later was fatal; he caught yellow fever in Panama.

was up, Jefferson Davis plowed ahead with his "scientific" evaluation of the various potential routes.

Benton's Buffalo Trail appeared to be out, not so much for its rough terrain, but because it crossed Paiute country. This hard fact became brutally apparent when the survey party was attacked on the banks of the Sevier River in Utah. In the worst defeat the Army had yet suffered in the West, eight men were slaughtered, including Captain John W. Gunnison, one of the country's most gifted explorers and engineers. The Gunnison disaster closed out the Buffalo Trail to serious consideration. As for the 35th Parallel Trail via Albuquerque, its chief surveyor, Lieutenant Amiel Weeks Whipple, submitted the staggering estimate of $169,210,265 as the cost of building there. Congress dismissed the route out of hand—only to discover later that a simple mathematical error on Lieutenant Whipple's part had added $75 million to the true cost.

From the Northern Trail, Governor Stevens reported that a railroad could be built for less than $96 mil-

lion. Moreover, he added modestly, the land compared favorably with the empire of Russia in its promise for the "cultivation of the great staples." Winter snows, he insisted, "would not present the slightest impediment to the passage of railroad trains." The man was such an irrepressible drumbeater, however, that his own territorial legislature commissioned an independent railroad survey as a check on the Governor's reliability. Even some of the members of Stevens' survey crew were skeptical. "A road *might* be built over the tops of the Himaleyah mountains," wrote George Suckley, a naturalist who had accompanied the Governor, "but no reasonable man would undertake it. I think the same of the Northern route."

Davis made the most of such doubts. In 1855 the Secretary of War announced his absolutely scientific and impartial recommendation to Congress: the Southern Trail. To buttress this foregone conclusion, Davis and his allies had been very busy rectifying a major embarrassment in the Southern Trail—namely, that it dipped below the Mexican border. Under the smoke screen of a little border-straightening, they introduced a bill in Congress authorizing James Gadsden, an emissary to Mexico—and sometime railroad promoter and South Carolina crony of Davis—to purchase sufficient land from Mexico to secure the necessary right of way. Benton quickly smelled the threat to his 38th parallel route. Did the government actually intend to spend money, he demanded on the floor of the House, for land "so utterly desolate, deserted, and God forsaken that Kit Carson says a wolf could not make his living on it?" And he saved a special barb for the United States Army: "It takes a grand national school like West Point to put national roads outside of a country and leave the interior without one."

In spite of such opposition, the Gadsden Treaty passed. But the final choice of where to locate a road was yet to be made. And by now the old sectional rivalries and jealousies, aggravated by the slavery question, had begun to harden into dangerous hostility between North and South. Hope of breaking the railroad deadlock was reserved for the time when the survey's completed findings would appear. And when that day finally came in 1860, no one could help being impressed by the lavish feast of data—13 whole volumes on the flora and fauna of the West, on the weather, the fisheries, the natural resources, on discoveries of interest to students of paleontology and geology, and on life among the Indians. Davis' Great Reconnaissance had indeed turned an educated eye on the remote and difficult places where railroads might go. But as an instrument to break a stalemate and establish a railroad, the reports were useless.

A particularly exasperated reader of the reports was a young civil engineer from Bridgeport, Connecticut, named Theodore Dehone Judah, one of two young men whose exhaustive field work would one day form the real bedrock of the transcontinental rail line. Judah had made his reputation by engineering the spectacular Niagara Gorge Railroad, and had completed a number of other important Eastern railroad projects, all before he was 28. During the spring of 1854 he was happily immersed in designing a new section of the Erie Railroad near Buffalo when he received an offer from Colonel Charles Wilson, president of the budding Sacramento Valley Railroad, to run a scientific survey

line for the road. Judah's wife, Anna, although she had learned to expect sudden changes by moving 20 times in the six years of her marriage, confessed to some consternation when her husband informed her by telegram, "We sail for California April 2."

Judah was both a dedicated railroader and an unquenchable optimist. Upon his arrival in Sacramento he dazzled his new employers by predicting a transcontinental future for their railroad, well before the Sacramento Valley's first locomotive—or even its first iron tracks—were shipped around the Horn. As he began work on the first 22-mile stretch from downtown Sacramento to the scruffy staging town of Folsom on the western slope of the Sierra, Judah referred to the project as the first leg of the "grand avenue of approach to the metropolis of the Pacific." But such optimism was premature. The gold mines above Folsom gave out just after Judah's road arrived and the populace around Folsom shriveled. In possession of a road going approximately nowhere, the railroad's directors suspended all further construction.

Judah turned to surveying for wagon roads to the silver towns of Nevada, which were attracting a new wave of treasure seekers. But railroads remained his obsession. After spending a summer exploring high passes in the Sierra, Judah returned to Sacramento and published a pamphlet called "A Practical Plan for Building the Pacific Railroad." In it he caustically dismissed the mass of irrelevant work that had been done before him, especially Davis' surveys.

"When a Boston capitalist is invited to invest in a railroad project," he wrote, "it is not considered sufficient to tell him that somebody has rode over the ground on horseback and pronounced it practicable. He does not care to be informed that there are 999 different varieties and species of plants and herbs, or that grass is abundant at this point; or buffalo scarce at that.

"His inquiries are somewhat more to the point. He wishes to know the length of your road. He says, let me see your map and profile, that I may judge of its alignment and grades. How many cubic yards of the various kinds of excavation and embankment have you, and upon what sections? Have you any tunnels, and what are their circumstances? How much masonry and where are your stone? How many bridges, river crossings, culverts, and what kind of foundations? How about timber and fuel? Where is the estimate of the cost of your road, and let me see its details?"

Judah himself was not yet in a position to answer such questions about a crossing of the Sierra. But he had no doubt that he would be. Anna Judah wrote that everything her husband did was in the interest of "the great continental Pacific railway. It was the burden of his thought day and night, largely of his conversation, till it used to be said, 'Judah's Pacific Railroad crazy,' and I would say, 'Theodore, those people don't care,' or 'you give your thunder away.' He'd laugh and say, 'But we must keep the ball rolling.'"

Judah made several trips to Washington, D.C., on behalf of California railroad promoters before 1860, and quickly became an accomplished Congressional buttonholer; indeed, he was such a success as a lobbyist that he was made clerk of both the House and Senate committees considering his Pacific railroad plan. But with Congress distracted by the specter of secession and perhaps war, even the spellbinding Judah could not force a decision on the railroad route. "The people are disposed to look with distrust upon grand speculations," he observed. Against the day when Congress would be more approachable, he resolved to go back to the Sierra and refine his explorations. By the fall of 1860, he was in the mountains with barometer and theodolite, looking for the perfect route across that awesome range.

He spent the rest of the summer vainly examining four known passes north of Lake Tahoe. Then, in response to a persuasive letter from an amateur surveyor named Daniel (Doc) Strong, who had read Judah's Pacific railroad pamphlet, Judah switched his explorations to the region around Donner Lake (named for the snowbound emigrant party that had starved there during the winter of '46). Strong was the pharmacist and, for lack of any other candidate, the doctor in the mining town of Dutch Flat in the Sierra foothills. In an effort to boost that town's commerce, he had charted a wagon route east from the town and across the Sierra crest. While so doing he had come upon a corridor through the crest far gentler than the old emigrant trace up to Donner Pass — a rocky obstacle course that had fallen into disuse a decade earlier. Now Strong wanted the support of a real surveyor for his discovery.

He took Judah afoot along a granite spur of unbroken regularity, the remnant of an ancient peneplain

Judah's first official map for the eastward-reaching Central Pacific *(red line)* was filed with the Secretary of the Interior on June 30, 1862 — the day before Lincoln signed the Pacific Railroad bill into law. The actual route, completed seven years later, hardly deviated from this early projection.

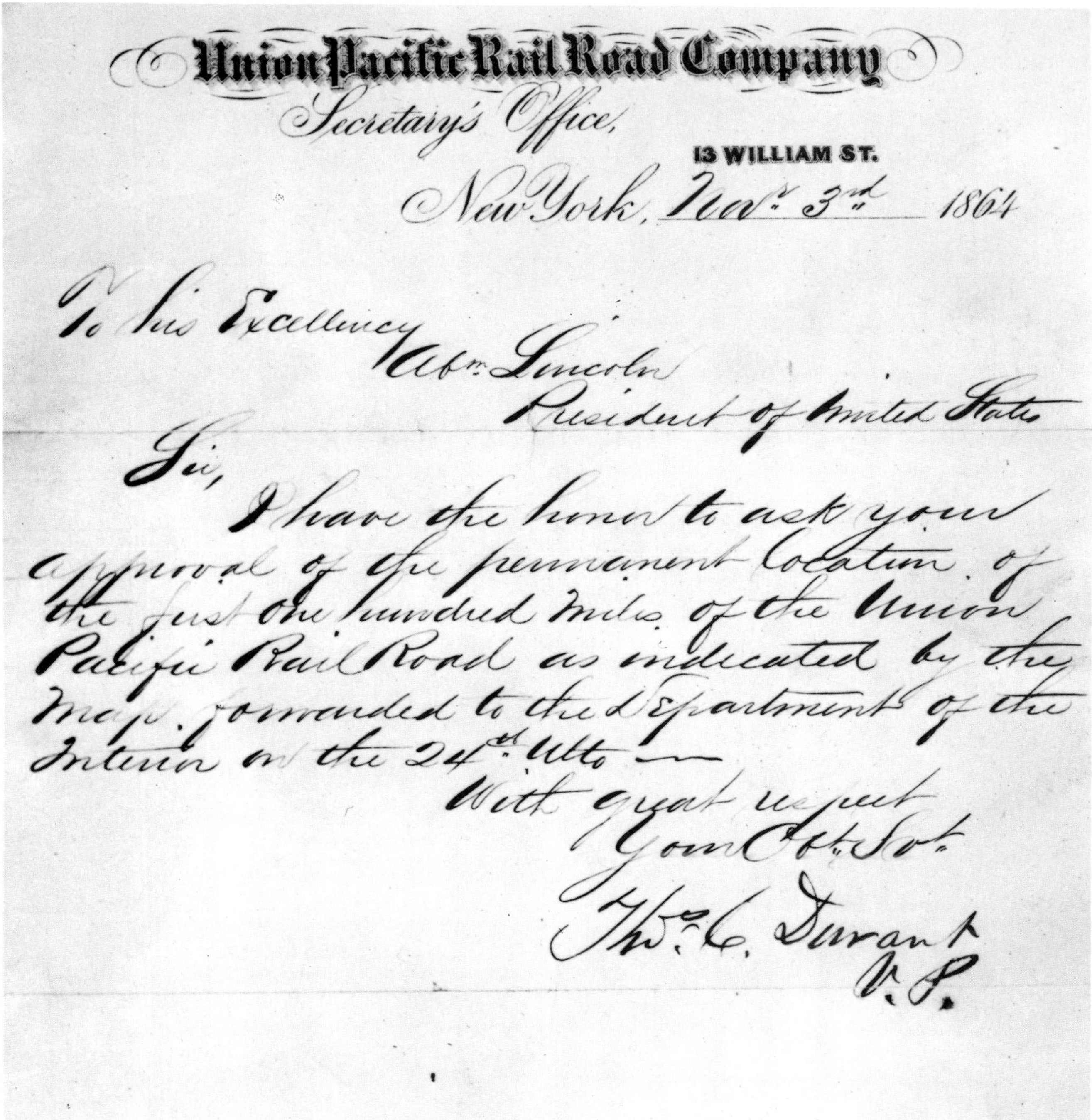

Union Pacific Rail Road Company
Secretary's Office,
13 WILLIAM ST.
New York, Nov. 3rd 1864

To His Excellency
Abr. Lincoln
President of United States

Sir,
I have the honor to ask your approval of the permanent location of the first one hundred miles of the Union Pacific Rail Road as indicated by the map forwarded to the Department of the Interior on the 24th Ulto —

With great respect
Your Obt. Sot.

Thos. C. Durant
V. P.

that rose steadily from a plateau between California's American and Yuba rivers all the way to the crest at the old emigrant pass. From there the route angled southeast along negotiable slopes to the Truckee River valley, and out onto the flats of the Great Basin. The two men explored the way in such excitement that a sudden snowstorm caught them at a high elevation, and they had to scramble down the steep mountainside in darkness. But Ted Judah knew that at last he had his route —not just for a wagon track but for a railroad through the mountains. Back in Doc Strong's drugstore, he sat down to work on his profiles and maps; then together he and Strong drew up the articles of association for the Pacific railroad.

Judah spent the next months furiously canvassing for investors, writhing in frustration at the reluctance of California's entrepreneurs to put up hard cash. "Not two years will go over the heads of these gentlemen," he told Anna, after one particularly discouraging bout of fund raising, "but that they will give up all they hope to have from their present enterprises to have what they put away tonight."

Judah was well accustomed to pitting his brains and will against other men's money, and at length he found

Judah, "you can have a wagon road if not a railroad."

Judah's detailed survey, done during the spring of 1861, proved a technical accomplishment of a very high order. When the road was finally built, no major changes were made in the line he projected. His ascent up the natural ramp to Donner Pass called for only a single 50-foot bridge over the Little Bear River. And his traverse over the summit was both simple and masterful: instead of dropping down the old emigrant trace in tortuous switchbacks, he ran an arcing line along the adjacent mountain flanks until he reached the gentler terrain of the Truckee valley.

Ted Judah was unabashedly proud. "The line over the mountains completes the first Western link of the Pacific Railroad," he wrote, in an echo of his earlier boast about the Sacramento line.

Despite this brilliant stroke, Judah's zealous impulses had led him into a few errors. He had calculated that the railroad would earn at least $100 million hauling cordwood to Sacramento from the forests along the right of way; no such profits ever materialized. He seriously underestimated the hazards of snow in the high Sierra *(pages 12-13);* and C. P. Huntington groused that when it came to figuring the costs of excavation, Judah often saw dirt where there was stone.

Judah remained unshaken in his optimism. Even the Humboldt River, a dying alkaline stream along which some silver strikes had been made, could inspire him. "It will not be many years before the new State of Humboldt will apply for admission into the Union," he promised in his rosy prospectus for the Central Pacific. And his prediction was only one in a prospectus that contained no less than 30 glowing promises.

When Judah came down from the mountain and returned to Washington, he found that momentous events had all but cleared the track for his transcontinental rail plan. Fort Sumter had been fired upon, and the outbreak of the Civil War had removed Jeff Davis and all other backing for the proposed southern route.

Just as important, perhaps, for Judah's crusade, he discovered that another tireless, talented young man named Grenville M. Dodge — whose railroading achievements ultimately would outstrip Judah's own — had privately surveyed in some detail the Platte valley emigrant route running west from Omaha and Council Bluffs, past the Rocky Mountains and on toward Salt Lake. ◉

seven men who, in their guarded fashion, were willing to pay for a confirming survey of the Dutch Flat route. It would cost about $35,000, Judah told them.

Principal among the seven were the four Sacramento merchants who were to become known as the Central Pacific Railroad's Big Four — Collis P. Huntington and Mark Hopkins, partners in a hardware store; a wholesale grocer named Leland Stanford; and Charles Crocker, who dealt in dry goods. Judah cajoled these cautious shopkeepers by arguing that a rail line would give them a trade monopoly in the Nevada mining districts. And should they decide to shoot for less, "Why," said

An elegant detachment of soldiers fires cannon salutes as the *Best Friend of Charleston* clatters along the track in South Carolina.

From puny puffers to transcontinental workhorses

On January 15, 1831, as pretty girls tossed flowers onto the track and the gentlemen in the rail coaches — mainly stockholders — cheered, America's first passenger locomotive wheezed out of Charleston, South Carolina. For six months the machine *(above),* named the *Best Friend of Charleston,* rattled at 20 mph between the city and nearby towns. Then one day its fireman, annoyed by the hiss of escaping steam, fastened down the engine's safety valve, thus ending its vital protective function.

Friend and fireman blew up together.

America's other early engines had sadly similar records. Called puffers for the sound they made, they spewed sparks, jerked people off their seats when the cars crashed forward at stops, and tended to jump the track when their rigid drive wheels hit a sharp curve.

But as the locomotives on these pages show, improvements came quickly. By 1833, engine design incorporated a swiveling front wheel assembly, a truck, to help ease a locomotive

around a bend. A funnel-shaped casing with a wire screen inside was fitted atop the stack to hold in cinders *(right).*

Four years later Henry Campbell united these and other improvements in an eight-wheel design like that below. Railroaders classify engines by wheel arrangements; this engine was a 4-4-0, meaning it had four wheels on its lead truck, four drivers and no wheels underneath the cab. It was this engine that, combining speed and power, conquered the first transcontinental route.

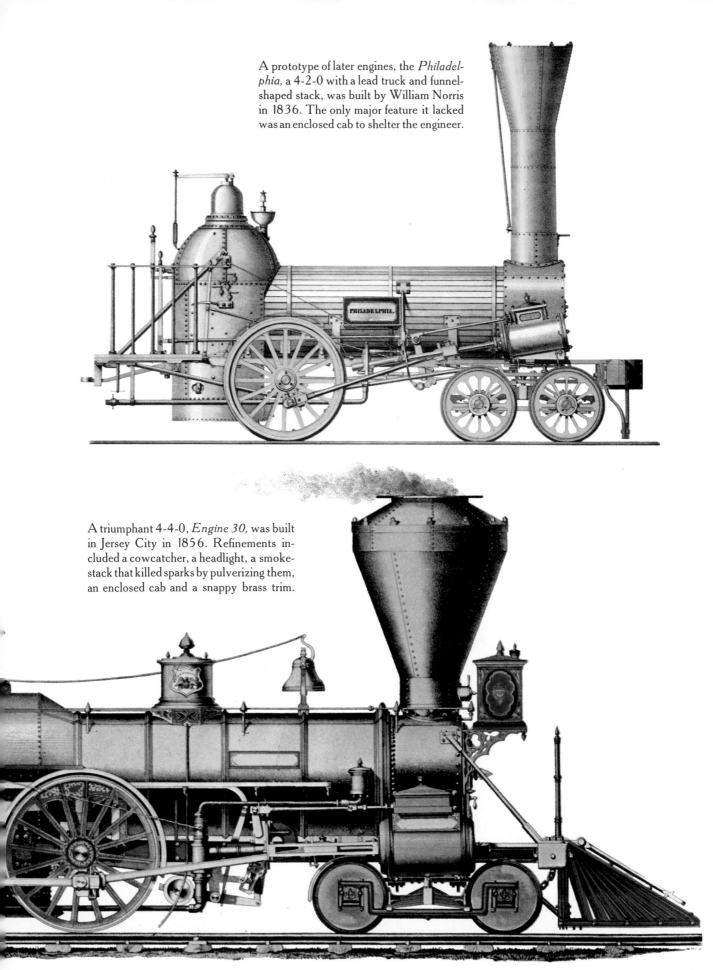

A prototype of later engines, the *Philadelphia,* a 4-2-0 with a lead truck and funnel-shaped stack, was built by William Norris in 1836. The only major feature it lacked was an enclosed cab to shelter the engineer.

A triumphant 4-4-0, *Engine 30,* was built in Jersey City in 1856. Refinements included a cowcatcher, a headlight, a smokestack that killed sparks by pulverizing them, an enclosed cab and a snappy brass trim.

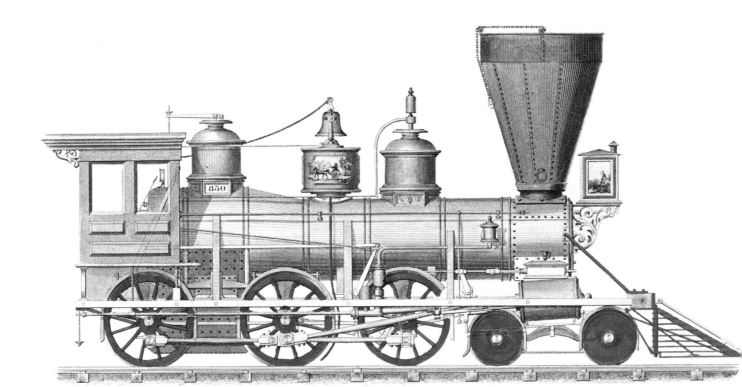

By the early 1860s, longer and more powerful locomotives began to compete with the 4-4-0. Some of the best came from the factory of Philadelphia's Matthias Baldwin, who built 1,500 engines during his career. His 10-wheeler, at top, was designed for both freight and passenger service, while the 0-8-0 at bottom hauled heavy freight. The latter applied its power through eight drivers.

Like Judah, Dodge was a New Englander. Like Judah, too, he had been well schooled in civil engineering before he moved west via Peru, Illinois, at age 20 in 1851. In Peru, Dodge had taken work as a surveyor for the Illinois Central, and right away he fell in love with the outdoor life. The young prodigy wrote home to his family that his memory of life in Massachusetts had become "a stench in my nostrils." He was a new-made man in this free place where, as if by magic, "lands wild and uncultivated have been subdued, fenced and cultivated."

Moving westward with the rails, Dodge next joined the Rock Island road, where he served an invaluable apprenticeship under Chief Engineer Peter A. Dey, one of the top engineers and surveyors in the field at that time. There, too, he made the important acquaintance of the ingenious promoter and Rock Island executive Thomas Durant, who had already begun formulating his plans for a transcontinental line. Dodge was delighted when Durant assigned him to start running a survey westward from Council Bluffs, Iowa, going as far as the foothills of the Rockies.

The young surveyor spent almost five years exploring the great Platte River valley, first for Durant but eventually for his own pleasure. He headed up into the Rockies and trailed back through the valleys, charting, reckoning, trading with Indians, living by his wits and good luck. He returned to Council Bluffs toward the end of the '50s, and produced a map of the Emigrant Trail that was widely circulated among Mormons and others who passed through town en route west.

When lawyer Abe Lincoln came to Council Bluffs in 1859 to inspect some property he was being offered as security for a loan, Dodge (at least according to his own somewhat suspect memoirs) was pointed out to him as the man who knew more than anybody about the land west of the river. Lincoln was already a knowledgeable railroad enthusiast, some of whose legal fees had come from work done on behalf of the Rock Island. And Dodge reported that, in an adept interrogation, the President-to-be "got all the information I'd collected" about possible transcontinental routes.

Sufficiently briefed on the Pacific railroad question, Lincoln returned to the more pressing business of the next year's Presidential campaign, and to the looming Civil War. As for Dodge, as soon as war broke out, he temporarily left off railroading to wangle a colonel's commission in the Union Army.

By now the whole country was aware that it had all the information it needed to pick the route of the long-promised Pacific railroad. Davis was gone and Benton was dead; as a consequence, no voices were left to speak against the route that had been most sensible all along: the basic path of the Emigrant Trail, the preferred route of both Dodge and Judah.

Congress could delay no longer. Plans had been drawn for the entire project; Judah and the Big Four were ready to build from California across the Sierra. Durant and his associates were champing at the bit on the eastern edge of the prairie. Suddenly it seemed a perfect disgrace that the Union was still weakened by the unspanned distance to the West, that emigrants still had to trudge the trail at a time when inventor George Pullman's sleeping cars were being run into Chicago.

The West was still as inaccessible by sea as it was by land. The 5,450-mile, 30-day voyage via an isthmus crossing at Panama was so expensive ($300) that few could afford it, and the risky, rough and terrible trip around Cape Horn often lasted six months. (The ocean voyage from New York to Calcutta was, in fact, easier, safer and hundreds of miles shorter than the 13,600-mile sail to San Francisco.) The distinguished 19th Century historian Hubert Howe Bancroft recorded the mood of the Far West in his *History of California:* "The sunburned immigrant, walking with his wife and little ones beside his gaunt and weary oxen in mid-continent, the sea-sick traveler, the homesick bride whose wedding trip had included a passage of the Isthmus, the merchant whose stock needed replenishing; everyone prayed for a Pacific Railroad."

The Pacific Railroad Act was passed in 1862, nine years after Jefferson Davis had been ordered to start the surveys, and on July 1, President Lincoln signed it into law. Two roads would be built, one from the West Coast, one from mid-continent; they would meet someplace in between.

Judah's prospectus (which he presented along with Anna's watercolor sketches of the scenery near Donner Pass) formed the basis of the charter that the bill awarded to the Central Pacific Railroad. The company would be given 10 miles of land in alternate sections on either side of its right of way for each mile of track laid, plus

Even in the scruffy bottoms of Utah's Weber Canyon, these Union Pacific surveyors rest easy in a snug campground of canvas tents.

Clinging to crevices, Union Pacific surveyors pass instruments up a cliff. In worse terrain they hoisted pack mules with block and tackle.

Veterans of campfire warbling, U.P. engineers of the Rocky Mountain Glee Club rehearse prior to a performance at a pioneer town.

48

Eleven husky surveyors line up over a primitive football in one of the first signal drills held on the Plains.

An engineer competes at checkers with a visiting railroad executive inside a handsomely appointed tent.

Northern Pacific engineers decorate their wagons en route to a celebration in a Minnesota town welcoming the coming of the railroad.

2 | Barons of the Western roads

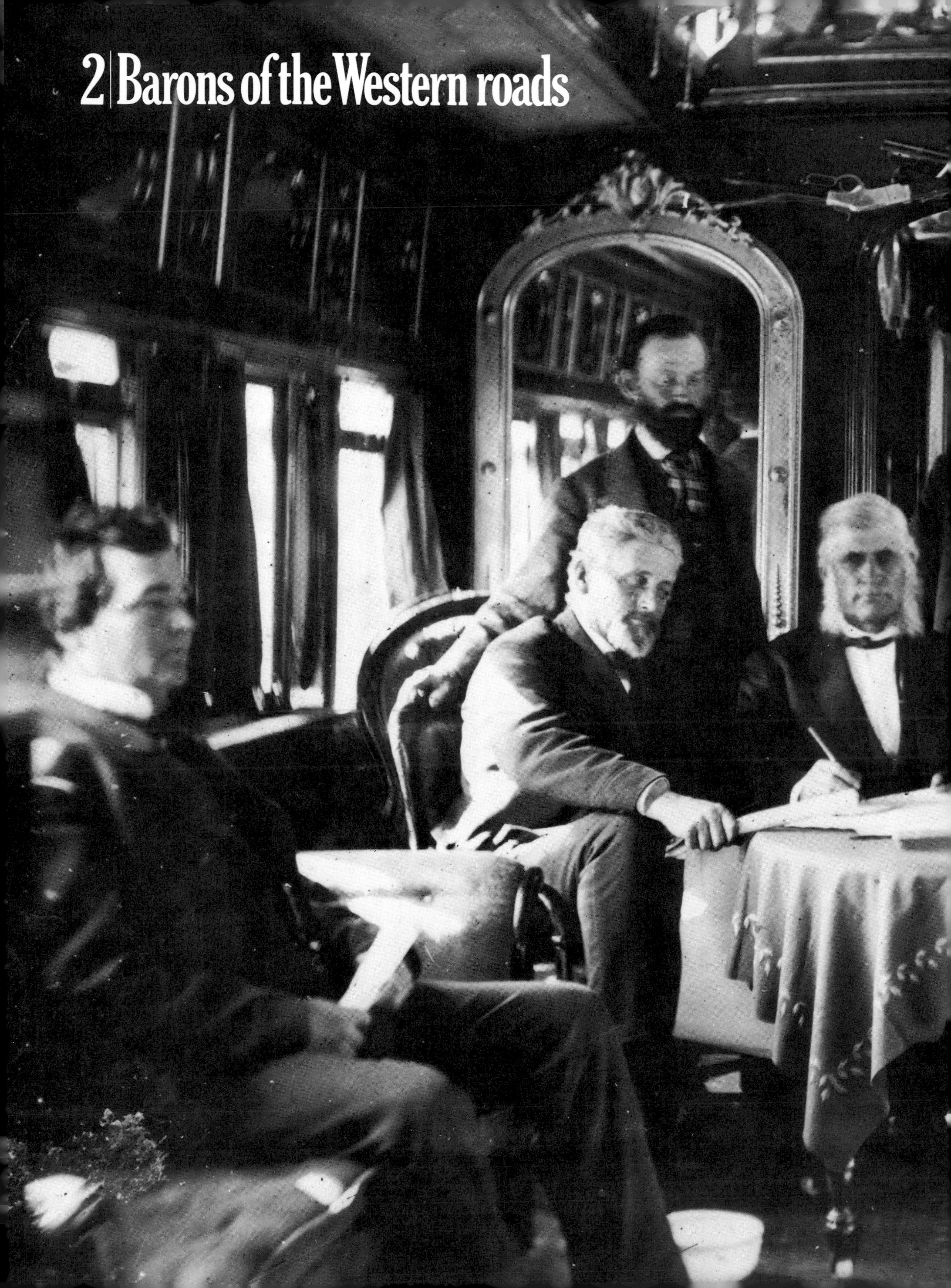

They epitomized the big men of their era, these Union Pacific entrepreneurs convened in the directors' private car. As solemn as deacons at a funeral, they surrounded themselves with heavy elegance—and spittoons—while they presided over the pioneering corporations, and the bald shenanigans, at the heart of railroad building in the Old West.

They were a diverse lot. Thomas Durant *(second from right)* was a medical school graduate who had gone into trade. Sidney Dillon, a water boy at age seven, had become entrenched in the money markets of New York. Among their counterparts on other roads, Leland Stanford, C. P. Huntington, Mark Hopkins and Charles Crocker of the Central Pacific started out as small-time California shopkeepers. And Cyrus K. Holliday of the Atchison, Topeka and Sante Fe was a lawyer from Pennsylvania who had become a founding father of Topeka, Kansas.

All shared a common talent for spanning the land with rails. To get the job done they scrounged for other people's money and, when they had to, risked their own. They cajoled Presidents and bought Congressmen. They did not hesitate to ruin old associates. Durant, the U.P.'s mastermind, was forced out once the railroad was completed. On the Northern Pacific, chief organizer Josiah Perham lost everything and died embittered before the road ran a train.

For all their fast dealing, they were the men who built the railroads that tied a vast nation together; perhaps more squeamish men would have failed.

Attended by two aides, Union Pacific bigwigs sit down to the conference table. From left they are: Silas Seymour, Sidney Dillon, Thomas C. Durant—the U.P.'s driving force—and John Duff. Construction chief Samuel Reed stands behind Durant.

INCORPORATED UNDER A SPECIAL ACT

OF THE STATE OF PENNSYLVANIA.

THE CREDIT MOBILIER OF AMERICA

ONE HUNDRED DOLLARS

PAR VALUE OF SHARES

Stamp

No. 58

45 SHARES

CAPITAL $ 2,500,000, IN 25,000 SHARES OF $ 100 EACH
WITH POWER TO INCREASE TO $ 10,000,000.

This Certifies that Union Pacific Ry Co.
is entitled to Four hundred fifty four Shares in the Capital Stock of the
Credit Mobilier of America on which have been paid 200 on
each share, transferable on the Books of the Company in person or by Attorney at the office of the Treasurer in the City of Philadelphia, or at any
Transfer Agency established by the Company, only upon surrender of this
Certificate and payment of all instalments then due.

Witness the signatures of the President and Secretary of the Company Dated at the
Transfer Agency in the City of New York this 18 day of December 1889

Benjamin F. Ham
auth Secretary

President.

CANCELLED

INCORPORATED OCTOBER 28, 1867

The Contract Finance Company

CAPITAL 5,000,000

50,000 SHARES $100 EACH

1000 SHARES

SACRAMENTO May 5th 1868

This Certifies that Leland Stanford
is the owner of One thousand Shares
in the **CAPITAL STOCK** of the **CONTRACT & FINANCE COMPANY**
Transferable only on the books of the Company by surrender of this
Certificate properly endorsed

In Testimony Whereof the said Company have caused this
Certificate to be signed by their President and Secretary.

W. E. Brown
SECRETARY

C. Crocker
PRESIDENT

Lith. Britton & Rey, San Francisco.

The "giveaway" that gave America the West

In the early spring of 1864, Mr. Collis P. Huntington of Sacramento and Dr. Thomas C. Durant of New York City went to Washington to get themselves some money, and maybe a few helpful friends in Congress. Both men were budding transcontinental railroad tycoons—Mr. Huntington with the Central Pacific Railroad, which was then heading eastward from Sacramento; Dr. Durant with the Union Pacific, bound west from Omaha. And both of them were in bad trouble.

For almost two years, in the midst of the Civil War, these men had been trying to realize a great national dream. The West and the East yearned for a rail line that would join the two halves of the continent. The routes of the line had already been mapped, across some 2,000 miles of grim and dusty wilderness, during the brilliant surveys of Theodore Judah and Grenville Dodge. Congress itself had chartered the road in the Railroad Act of 1862, which held out the promise of free land and government loans once construction got underway. In separate negotiations, the railroad agreed to carry mail, government supplies and troops at low rates. The road had found no less a champion than President Abraham Lincoln, who saw it as a solid and enduring foundation for national unity. But despite these high credentials and the good will of the entire nation,

> *I give no grudging vote in giving away either money or land. I would sink $100 million to build the road and do it most cheerfully and think I had done a great thing for my country. What are $75 million or $100 million in opening a railroad across regions of this continent that shall connect the people of the Atlantic and the Pacific and bind us together. Nothing! As to the lands, I don't begrudge them.*
>
> SENATOR HENRY WILSON, 1862

the railroad planners were stymied.

The problem was money. Both Huntington's C.P. and Durant's U.P. existed as joint stock companies, empowered to raise cash by selling stocks and bonds to the public. But in those turbulent Civil War years, when a man could get rich overnight peddling guns to the Union Army, no sober-minded investor wanted to risk his capital on such a wildcat scheme. A rail line through the wilderness—who would ever ride it? Yet more money would be needed to build it than had ever been spent, in all the annals of high finance, on a single enterprise. More than $100 million would have to be raised, an amount almost twice as large as the total federal budget in the first year of the Civil War. To most investors, the project seemed as visionary and improbable as a voyage to the moon.

So the most ambitious undertaking of the century languished for want of cash. After little more than a year of construction, the Central Pacific's funds were depleted. Work had slowed to a standstill with less than 20 miles of track laid—half the distance needed to qualify for government aid under the Railroad Act. As for the Union Pacific, its groundbreaking ceremonies the previous December had drained its treasury dry. The U.P. had yet to get outside Omaha's city limits.

This was the state of affairs that had brought the two aspiring railroad tycoons to Washington. Both men had put their modest personal fortunes on the line, Huntington borrowing heavily against his Sacramento hardware business, Durant plunging into U.P. stock with money he had made from railroad ventures in the Midwest. Now, with the last of their funds, they hoped to pry more generous loans and land allotments from Con-

---

Stock certificates in the Credit Mobilier and the Contract & Finance Company brought huge profits to their holders — who also ran the Union Pacific and Central Pacific. The roads awarded vastly inflated contracts to these construction companies.

the Central Pacific more than $1 million in increased federal loans for laying track across the "difficult terrain" of the nearly flat Sacramento valley.

Even this infusion of government aid was not enough to pull the Central Pacific out of the red. At least $12.5 million would be needed before Governor Stanford's "great highway of nations" extended farther than a good buggy ride from Sacramento. No one realized this more keenly than Huntington, who soon emerged as the mastermind of the four partners. For one thing, government aid came in greenbacks, which nobody out West trusted. The railroad would be hit with heavy discounts, sometimes as severe as 57 cents on the dollar, in converting them into gold. Also, as the C.P.'s purchasing agent, Huntington found his monetary woes compounded by the problems of a war-torn nation.

One of these national problems was inflation. When Huntington was forced to pay $13,688 for the C.P.'s first locomotive, a small engine with two pairs of drive wheels, he sank into the dark mood of a trader who reckons he has been taken: before the war the cost of a much larger locomotive had been $10,000. His spirits were not improved when he learned that a ton of rails had soared in price from $55 to $115 since 1861 — and that was just the cost at the Boston wharf, with freight charges for the trip around Cape Horn still to come. The war effort was straining every mill and forge, and Huntington often had to invoke the patriotic thunder of the old railroad debates before he could place orders at any price. Even then, there was always the risk that the rails, spikes, shovels, wheelbarrows, hammers and countless other items that Crocker was frantically calling for in California would be impounded by the War Department and sent off for use against the South.

On one occasion the need for a locomotive became so acute that Huntington could not wait for the normal six-month journey round the Horn. He had an engine disassembled on the East Coast, shipped to Panama by steamer, loaded on flatcars and sent over the Isthmus by railroad, loaded again on a Pacific steamer and shipped to San Francisco, where lighters were waiting to carry it up the Sacramento River. The whole trip took only 35 days — but in freight charges alone, the transaction cost Huntington $37,000.

With expenses like these facing them every day, the C.P. partners were hard pressed to keep going. Stan-

ford tried to sell C.P. securities to a syndicate of local investors, only to be turned down on all sides. There was a time, Crocker said in later years, when he "would have been glad to take a clean shirt and get out." And so Huntington, whom the others deferred to in all matters of finance, had gone east to the great money capitals of Boston and New York in search of new funds. Taking powers of attorney from his partners in order to pledge their assets as the need arose, he had left for New York early in 1863. Upon his arrival he announced with commendable bravado that shares in his great adventure were available to the serious investor in block lots of no less than $1.5 million.

The offer was greeted by deep silence.

It did not raise Huntington's spirits to know that Dr. Thomas Durant of the Union Pacific, his rival in the building of a transcontinental road, was having his troubles, too. After six months, only $300,000 worth of U.P. shares had been sold. In their attempts to raise capital in Eastern money markets, Huntington and Durant were learning the hard way that the financial community still looked upon the Western railroad venture as a poor risk — and a long-range risk at that. The line would take years to build. How could it offer the quick and easy profits that financiers were raking in from the Civil War boom in munitions, metals, provisions and every other kind of war matériel? And the huge land grants promised by the government produced colossal yawns from Eastern money brokers; the land was well-nigh worthless until a railroad could be built across it. How many years would pass, investors asked themselves, before the title to those land-grant acres would be worth anything on the market?

Yet, the affairs of the Union Pacific took a different course from those of the C.P. For one thing, Thomas

---

THE MEN BEHIND THE CENTRAL PACIFIC

Of these eight somber Central Pacific officers, who parlayed $150,000 cash into construction profits of over $200 million, four were founders of the company: Leland Stanford, president; C. P. Huntington, vice president; Mark Hopkins, treasurer; and Charles Crocker, president of the C.P.'s lucrative construction company. By the mid-'60s, the top management also included Samuel Montague, chief engineer; Edwin Crocker (Charles's brother), attorney; Edward Miller Jr., secretary; and Benjamin Redding, who handled some 17.5 million acres in C.P. real estate deals.

OFFICERS OF THE CENTRAL PACIFIC RAIL ROAD

The Central Pacific's first locomotive, the wood-burning *Governor Stanford,* began hauling passengers on April 26, 1864, from Sacramento to Roseville — an 18½-mile trip. The one-way fare was $1.85.

The C.P.'s first annual report *(right)* listed $8.5 million in capital stock — but could show cash assets of only $24,620. Before construction of the road could begin, the partners had to contribute $34,500 each.

Durant seemed undismayed by his failure to lure private capital. The Doctor, as everyone called him, addressed himself to the Union Pacific's troubled affairs in an atmosphere of absolute certainty and worldly affluence. His splendid manners and his princely wardrobe, his French-speaking friends and his love of fine wines, the rococo elegance of the statues and potted palms and caged canaries that crowded his office — all these left no room for doubt, the Doctor was a virtuoso. He was also an old hand at railroad promotions. Abandoning both his medical education and his family's flour and grain business in New York, he had moved West as early as 1851 to help build the Michigan Southern and the Chicago & Rock Island lines. Later he had sent 22-year-old Grenville Dodge, then a young surveyor just beginning the first of his several railroad careers, into the Platte River valley to scout locations for the Mississippi & Missouri — a transcontinental road that never came near to completion.

Durant had known the good days of the business and the bad days of the business, and the bad days seemed to suit him best; he was a man for difficult mo-

ments. And this was a moment when the future of the transcontinental railroad (or at least the eastern half of it) hung upon the Doctor's ingenuity. It inspired him to some financial sleight of hand that he forever afterward regarded as the master stroke of his career.

As set up by Congress, the U.P.'s charter required that $2 million in stock had to be subscribed before the company could begin operations — and he had sold only $300,000 worth. Very well, then, he would work up a sales pitch so tempting that not even the most hard-nosed prospect could resist it. The deal was simplicity itself. A 10 per cent down payment in cash was required by law for every purchase of U.P. stock. Durant decided he would put up the 10 per cent himself as a loan to any investor willing to buy. Durant agreed to take all the risk; an investor could one day either pay him back and take over the stock, or he could let it go and trust the Doctor to assume full ownership.

It was a bravura stroke, and it worked. Durant later said, "I got my friends to make up subscriptions to the amount of $2,180,000 by furnishing three-fourths of the money myself." In the process, he also grabbed con-

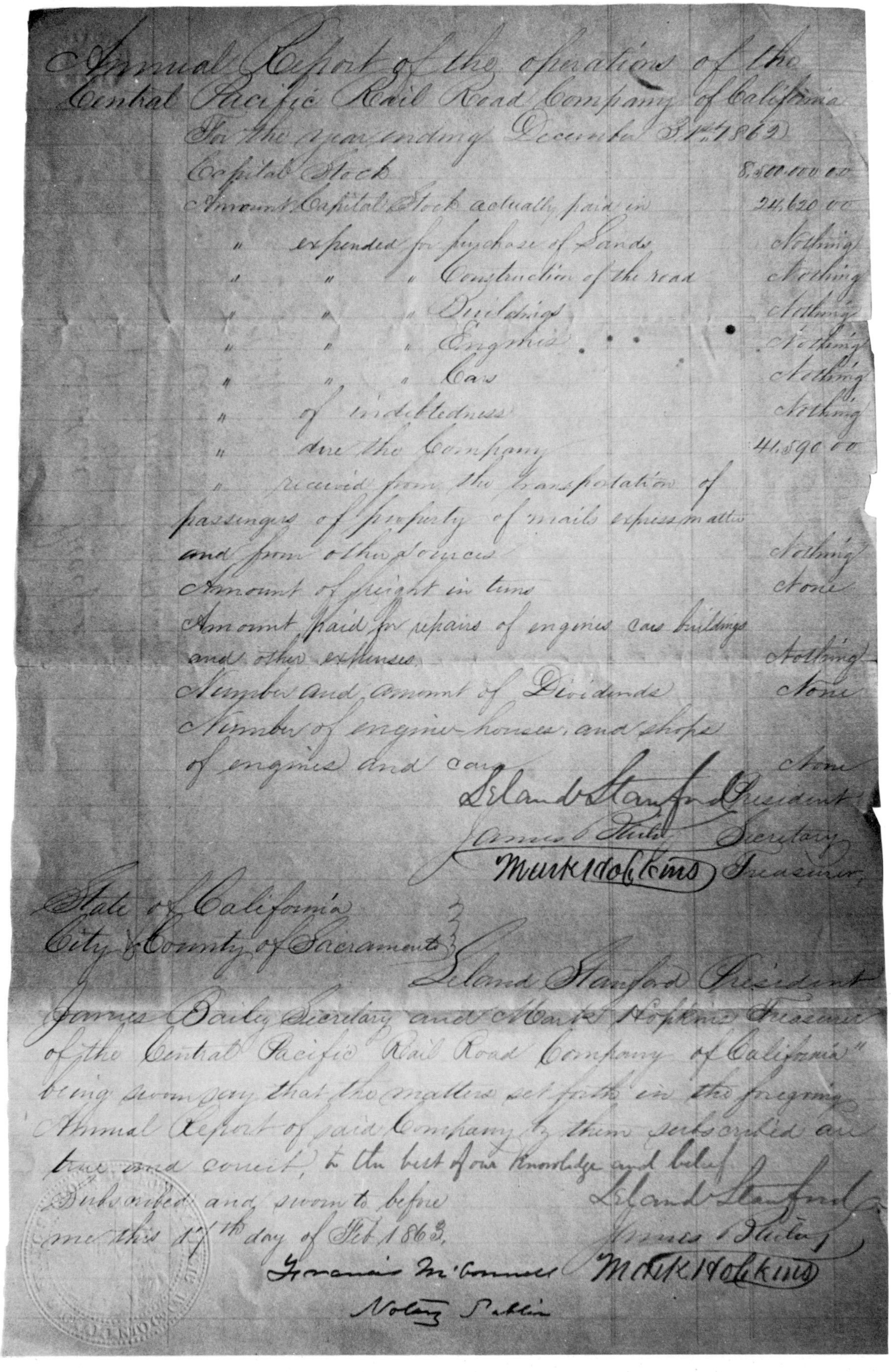

Annual Report of the operations of the
Central Pacific Rail Road Company of California
For the year ending December 31st 1862

Capital Stock	8,500,000 00
Amount Capital Stock actually paid in	24,620 00
" expended for purchase of Lands	Nothing
" " " Construction of the road	Nothing
" " " Buildings	Nothing
" " " Engines	Nothing
" " " Cars	Nothing
" of indebtedness	Nothing
" due the Company	41,590 00
" received from the transportation of passengers of property of mails express matter and from other sources	Nothing
Amount of freight in tons	None
Amount paid for repairs of engines cars buildings and other expenses	Nothing
Number and Amount of Dividends	None
Number of engine houses, and shops of engines and cars	None

Leland Stanford President
James Bailey Secretary
Mark Hopkins Treasurer

State of California
City & County of Sacramento

Leland Stanford President
James Bailey Secretary and Mark Hopkins Treasurer
of the Central Pacific Rail Road Company of California"
being sworn say that the matters set forth in the foregoing
Annual Report of said Company by them subscribed are
true and correct, to the best of our knowledge and belief

Subscribed and sworn to before
me this 17th day of Feb 1863.

Leland Stanford
James Bailey
Mark Hopkins

Francis McConnell
Notary Public

Central Pacific officer Charles Crocker set his name to this come-on for a road through the mining town of Dutch Flat. Built to move supplies for the railroad, it soon became a toll road and bonanza for the C.P.

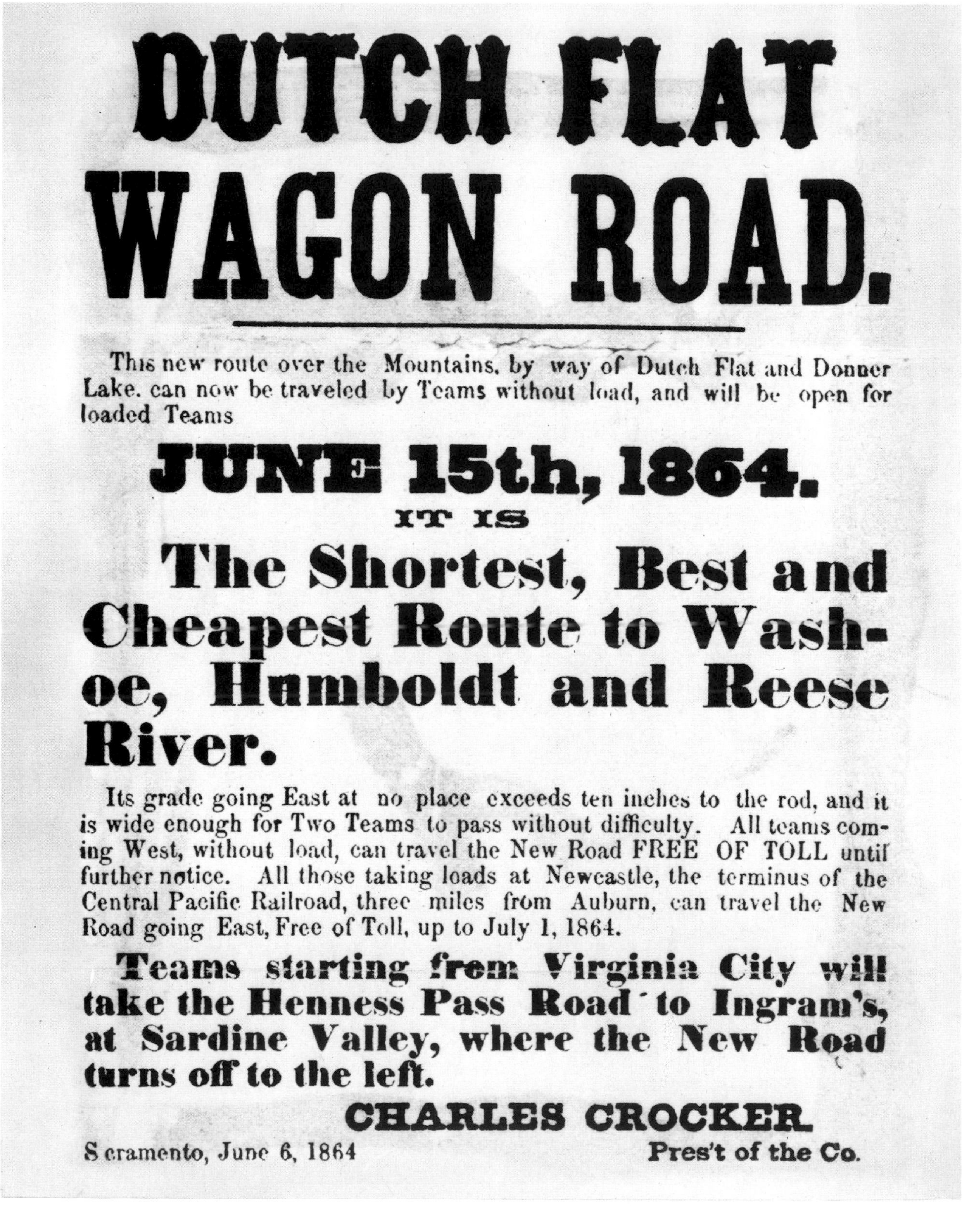

DUTCH FLAT WAGON ROAD.

This new route over the Mountains, by way of Dutch Flat and Donner Lake, can now be traveled by Teams without load, and will be open for loaded Teams

JUNE 15th, 1864.

IT IS

The Shortest, Best and Cheapest Route to Washoe, Humboldt and Reese River.

Its grade going East at no place exceeds ten inches to the rod, and it is wide enough for Two Teams to pass without difficulty. All teams coming West, without load, can travel the New Road FREE OF TOLL until further notice. All those taking loads at Newcastle, the terminus of the Central Pacific Railroad, three miles from Auburn, can travel the New Road going East, Free of Toll, up to July 1, 1864.

Teams starting from Virginia City will take the Henness Pass Road to Ingram's, at Sardine Valley, where the New Road turns off to the left.

CHARLES CROCKER.

Sacramento, June 6, 1864   Pres't of the Co.

trol of the U.P. for himself. Though the company charter restricted to 200 shares the amount of stock that any individual could own, Durant wound up with 750. Flushed with success, he turned to Washington, where Congress and the executive might be persuaded to sweeten up the Railroad Act. The Doctor was ready to start some high, wide and handsome lobbying.

So was Collis Huntington. After six months in New York and Boston, he had unloaded a mere $250,000 in Central Pacific bonds—and even then he had to give his personal guarantee for the interest. It must have pained Huntington, who hated to part with a dime unnecessarily, to consort with Congressmen; he later called them "the hungriest group of men who ever got together." But he saw that there was nothing else for it but to go down to Washington and get to work.

Huntington was still a comparative amateur at high-level flimflam; only a year before he had thought it wise to pay two cloakroom sharks $11,000 to coach him in the art of lobbying. Now, in the spring of 1864, he scraped together his dwindling supply of cash and took it with him to Washington to foster understanding of his company's plight. Typically Dr. Durant operated on a more lavish scale: he managed to provide himself with a delicately titled "suspense fund" of half a million dollars. The turning point had been reached. From now on, behavior of both men would be (as one anonymous wit said of Huntington) "scrupulously dishonest."

There is, nevertheless, a sympathetic case to be made for the railroad barons of the 1860s, and especially for those majestically avaricious men who got rich building the nation's first transcontinental railroad: the Big Four of the Central Pacific, and the inside ring that ran the Union Pacific. These early empire builders were, indeed, everything their enemies called them: ruthless, rapacious, treacherous, greedy and grasping. But they were men of their time, America's Gilded Age, when business ethics, and morality itself, had reached a state of giddy upheaval. Immense fortunes were amassed by the shoddiest methods. Quick money and wholesale corruption in government were the price of the Civil War industrial boom. "Even in this time of trial," lamented General Sherman, "cheating in clothes, blankets, flour, bread, everything, is universal." It was an era when one of the most blatant scoundrels in American history, New York jobber Jim Fisk, could say with a

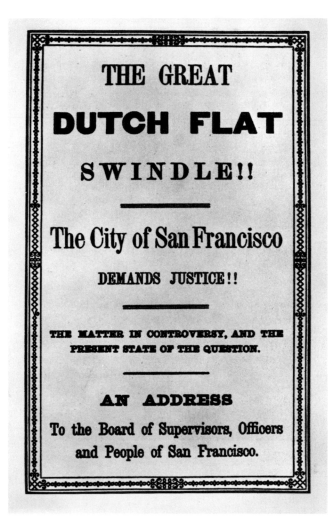

THE GREAT
DUTCH FLAT
SWINDLE!!

The City of San Francisco

DEMANDS JUSTICE!!

THE MATTER IN CONTROVERSY, AND THE
PRESENT STATE OF THE QUESTION.

AN ADDRESS

To the Board of Supervisors, Officers
and People of San Francisco.

grin, "You can sell anything to the government at almost any price you've got the guts to ask." And later Fisk, with his equally notorious partner, Jay Gould, would defraud the public of $64 million by watering the stock of their Erie Railroad in New York, flee town when discovered and then return to run the railroad.

America, though shocked at such tactics, gave the railroad barons a begrudging respect. "Ruthless as a crocodile," one newsman described Collis Huntington, and he meant it as a compliment. Even high abuse did not ruffle the barons. Charles Crocker, when lambasted by a business rival as "a living, breathing, waddling monument to the triumph of vulgarity, viciousness and dishonesty," was so impressed by the man's eloquence that he hired him for his railroad. It was all part of a game, played for enormous stakes, that hinged on the

Rewards for the rail barons were rich and quick, as this painting of bearded C.P. President Leland Stanford (seated to left of tree) shows.

66

Surrounded by friends and family, Stanford here enjoys the good life at the 1,700-acre Palo Alto farm he acquired from his rail earnings.

Horatio Alger virtues of working and winning. And in their own eyes, the railroad barons were no more wicked than destiny directed them to be.

The concept of destiny was enough to bring out the brigand in the mildest of these men. Like John D. Rockefeller, Andrew Carnegie and other high achievers of their age, the railroad barons were profoundly in tune with the teachings of the English philosopher Herbert Spencer—and his definition of destiny did not encompass the humble destiny of the poor. Borrowing freely from the recently published findings of Charles Darwin, Spencer elevated to the status of a cosmic law the simple urge of the rich to get richer. He argued that the pursuit of wealth by a spirited few was the major process by which a civilization perfected itself. This view of life, which came to be called Social Darwinism, made avarice a virtue, or at worst a heroic excess; it dismissed traditional business ethics as a tame, inadequate approach to life's great contest. Fierce, unrelenting competition, Spencer preached, was the only mechanism that fulfilled the harsh terms of natural selection. A true Spencerian, it was said, would fire his lame office boy and congratulate himself for aiding evolution.

This creed held a special appeal for the railroad barons—almost all of whom had made their first small fortunes as merchants or traders, then entered realms of enterprise that had not existed before their time. Herbert Spencer himself saw the railroad as a magnificent historical force that would unite distant peoples and put an end to tribalism and hatred. The barons might not have studied him closely enough to illuminate their actions by that concept—but when it came to discharging their evolutionary duty to get a leg up on the other fellow, they could hardly have been more steadfast.

So it was to be expected that, in the spring of 1864, Collis Huntington and Thomas Durant, two men of utterly different style and disposition, were both directed by destiny to go to Washington with bundles of cash to buy themselves some votes. By the time they had disbursed their educational funds in the corridors of the Capitol, all but a few querulous Congressmen were ready to make some improvements upon the Railroad Act of 1862. Huntington and Durant already had the support of Abraham Lincoln, made manifestly clear in any number of public statements. With the legislative and executive branches in happy concord, a new bill, the

Pacific Railroad Act of 1864, sailed through Congress and was signed by the President.

It was a model of openhandedness. Land grants to the two roads were doubled: from the original 10 square miles to 20, in alternate sections, for each mile of track they laid. Eventually the C.P. and U.P. would get a total of almost 21 million acres, or more land than Vermont, Massachusetts and Connecticut put together. More significant, the federal loans of $32,000 and $48,000 a mile for the long stretch between the Rockies and the western base of the Sierra would not be deferred until the railroad companies actually laid track upon it. Instead, as soon as each 20 miles of roadbed had been prepared, two thirds of the money would be released. Here at last was an opportunity to take the ready cash and start building in earnest. Since no meeting point was established for the C.P. and U.P. track, the railroad builders got set for a hell-for-leather race to fling the most mileage across the continent.

Yet, for a time, that race infuriatingly refused to get started. The Act of 1864 turned the C.P. and the U.P. into land-holding companies of enormous potential wealth. But private investors were still skittish. "Building a railroad from nowhere to nowhere at public expense is not a legitimate enterprise," snorted Commodore Cornelius Vanderbilt, who was busily engaged in grabbing control of the privately financed New York Central and Erie lines between New York City and Chicago. Most Easterners agreed with the commodore.

At last a tiny measure of progress was achieved by the Central Pacific. Through Huntington's continual pledging of his personal credit the C.P. found the money for token construction. Later Huntington boasted that he had signed notes for $7 million—far more money than he owned up to that point in his life—before he was sure that his line would ever cross the Sierra.

By June of 1864 the road was earning a dime a mile hauling passengers over exactly 31 miles of track between Sacramento and Newcastle. Not much, but enough to qualify for the first government loans. On the other hand, the Union Pacific's affairs seemed hopelessly mired down: the Civil War ended without a foot of U.P. track getting past the city limit of Omaha—or Bilksville, as many had taken to calling it.

Abraham Lincoln had been disgruntled by the U.P.'s failure to get underway. A few weeks before his assas-

Thomas Durant, vice president and chief architect of the Union Pacific's elaborate corporate structure, oversaw the financing of the road's construction — and made sure a good share of the money came his way.

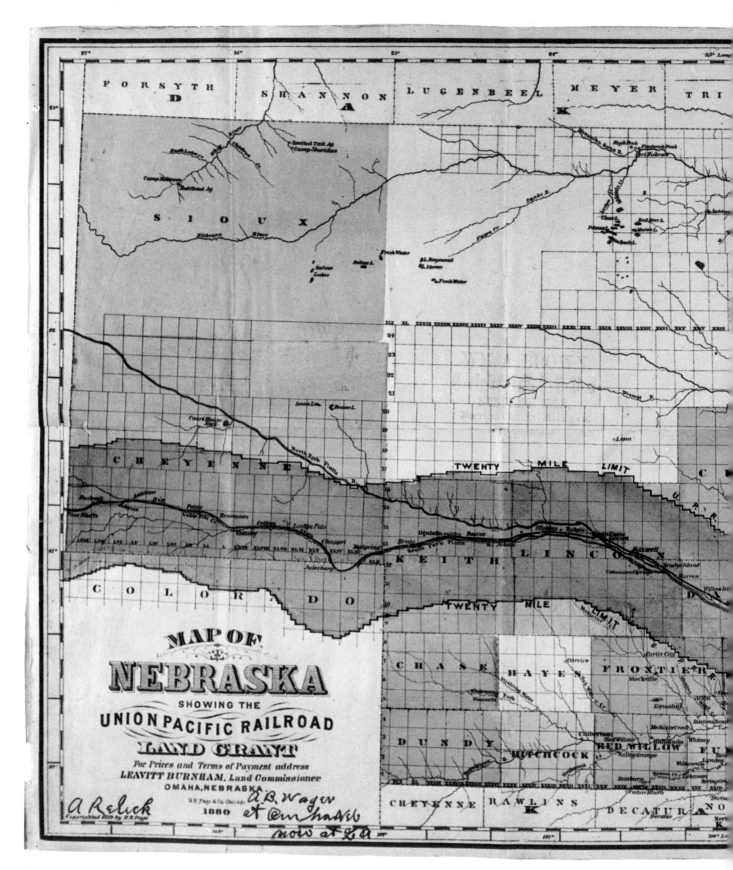

Promoting land sales along the strip granted by the federal government, the Union Pacific passed out this map showing the limits of its holdings in Nebraska. Although the opponents of land grants blasted the government's giveaway of nearly five million acres in Nebraska

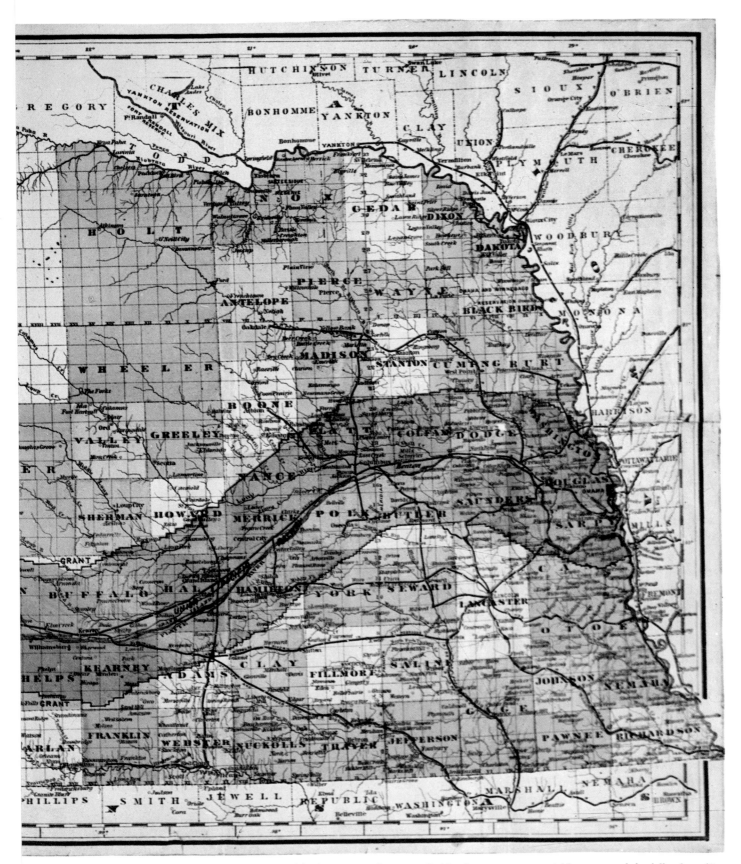

alone (almost a tenth of all the land in the state), the scheme proved most profitable: the government quickly recovered the full value of its land grants by retaining every other square-mile section along the right of way, then selling them for a minimum price of $2.50 an acre.

To help guide the U.P., Lincoln called in millionaire Oakes Ames *(right).* He and his brother, Oliver *(below),* took control of the U.P. by buying into the Credit Mobilier, which the U.P. secretly owned.

stock to help adjust the general to the new ways of railroading. Somehow the securities never arrived; the wily Durant forgot that part of the deal. Dodge, considerably miffed, had to buy the stock himself—and, with a careful eye to the future, he did so in his wife's name. Later on, when the financial affairs of the Union Pacific began to turn sour, Dodge would declare that he had never in his life owned a share of that stock.

But in 1866 Dodge's stock-dealing side had still to mature. Sometimes, as chief engineer, he found himself fighting Dey's old battle against the men who managed the railroad's finances, especially when they ordered him to run track in needless snakelike curves for the sake of increased loans *(pages 76-77).* Dodge fumed and sputtered as "Durant and those other thieves" routinely approved construction estimates that doubled the ones provided by his own staff. At times the U.P.'s bookkeepers would perform miracles of absentmindedness. Certain sections of track would be paid for more than once, each time at grossly inflated prices. The railroad's huge army of graders and tracklayers *(pages 82-89)* would be whipped along at a reckless clip, and every hammer laid to a spike would drive the Union Pa-

cific deeper into indebtedness to the Credit Mobilier.

The Credit Mobilier waxed fat. By the end of its fourth year, when its directors decided to peddle the stock to a few select buyers, they declared a dividend of almost 100 per cent. At last the transcontinental railroad project had something of immediate appeal to the Spencerian mind. Faith in the West was no longer a necessary part of a railroad baron's makeup: all he needed was the desire to lay track. With their built-in profit mills, railroads could be constructed for the sake of constructing railroads—never mind where they were bound.

The inner-ring scheme was by no means the exclusive property of Thomas Durant. Out in Sacramento, the Big Four set up a similar operation to milk the funds of the Central Pacific; their construction firm had the inscrutable name of the Contract & Finance Company, C. Crocker, President. It spilled such riches into the pockets of the four onetime shopkeepers that Crocker was able to plunk down $1,250,000 just to build himself a new house. But it was Durant who had started the winds of embezzlement blowing strong across the plains. And his example brought on a stampede of Western railroad promotions beginning about 1867.◉

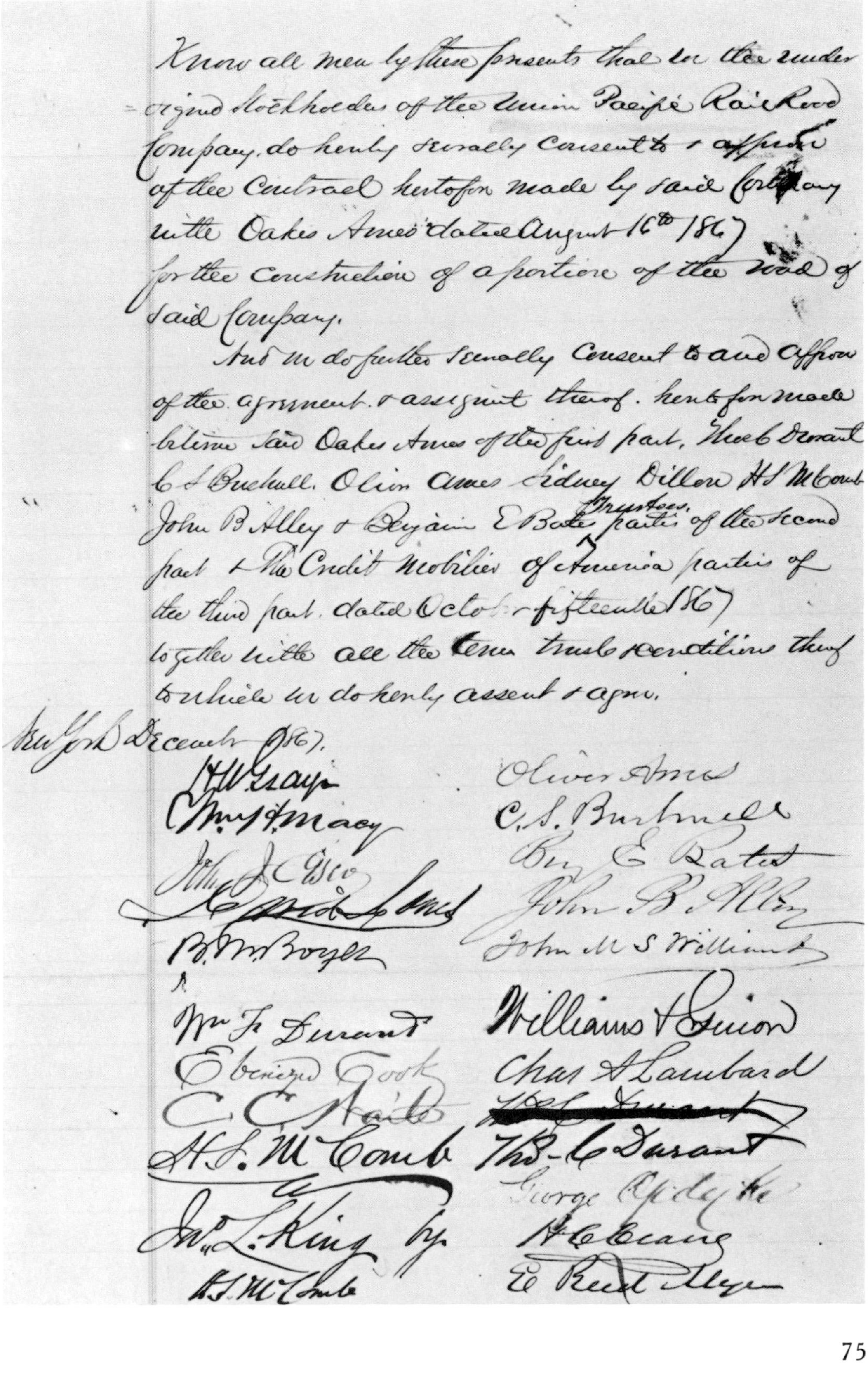

Know all men by these presents that we the under
=signed stockholders of the Union Pacific Rail Road
Company, do hereby severally consent to & approve
of the Contract heretofore made by said Company
with Oakes Ames dated August 16th 1867
for the construction of a portion of the road of
said Company.

And we do further severally consent to and approve
of the agreement & assignment thereof. heretofore made
between said Oakes Ames of the first part, Thos C Durant
C S Bushnell. Oliver Ames Sidney Dillon H S McComb
John B Alley & Benjamin E Bates parties of the second
part & The Credit Mobilier of America parties of
the third part. dated October fifteenth 1867
together with all the terms trusts & conditions thereof
to which we do hereby assent & agree.

New York December 1867.

[Signatures:]

Oliver Ames
C. S. Bushnell
Ben E Bates
John B Alley
John M S Williams
Williams & Guion
Chas H Lambard
Thos C Durant
George Opdyke
H C Crane
E Reed Myer

GRENVILLE DODGE
Chief Engineer, U.P.

SIDNEY DILLON
Director, U.P.

PHILIP SHERIDAN
General, U.S. Army

ULYSSES S. GRANT
Presidential nominee

WILLIAM T. SHERMAN
General, U.S. Army

Top brass from the Union Pacific and the Army meet at Fort Sanders, Wyoming Territory, under the aegis of Presidential candidate Ulysses S. Grant to settle a feud over the future routing of the railroad. Grenville Dodge, glowering at far left, had planned "a commercially economical line" — although he had not been above purchasing some Credit Mobilier stock in his wife's name. His adversary, Thomas Durant, had his eye on a more complex route that would bring in more government loans. Each accused the other of mismanagement. Grant, surrounded by old Army cronies — Generals Sherman and Sheridan, Indian-fighter Harney and Civil War hero Potter of the Union Army — listened dourly as Dodge threatened to quit if anyone tampered with his plans. Quickly Grant decided in Dodge's favor.

WILLIAM HARNEY
General, U.S. Army

THOMAS C. DURANT
Vice President, U.P.

JOSEPH POTTER
General, U.S. Army

The denouement of the railroad construction scandal came with the exposure by the New York *Sun* of the wheelings and dealings of the Credit Mobilier. A Congressional inquiry implicated many big names.

A railroad promoter could easily orchestrate an impressive clamor for the coming of his trains among settlers in almost any part of the West. Once he had done that, the expenditure of a modest sum among the legislators in Washington would normally suffice to get him land grants from the federal government. Thus, the Atlantic and Pacific Railroad received three million acres to build a line roughly following the Albuquerque Trail along the 35th parallel.

Thomas Scott of the Pennsylvania Railroad started a yet more ambitious Western line. Scott had already earned a reputation in the East as an adroit railroad lobbyist; in describing him, the political reformer Wendell Phillips said that "the members of twenty legislatures rustled like dry leaves in a winter wind as he trailed his garments across the country." When Scott descended upon Congress with suitable cash enticements, proposing to build the Texas & Pacific Railroad along the old Southern Trail, the well-paid legislators gave him 18 million acres.

All told, between 1850 and 1872, Congress and various state governments granted Western railroads 116 million acres — a total expanse of free land that measured twice the area of Utah. Yet, at the end of that period there was still only one thin line operating from the Mississippi to the Pacific. Meanwhile, railroad lobbyists had helped reduce the moral tone of an already knavish government by the constant pressure of graft, bribery and corruption. Collis Huntington alone was spending from $200,000 to $500,000 at every session of Congress. Recalling his outrage during those sessions, one honest Congressman, Job E. Stevenson of Ohio, said: "The House of Representatives was like an auction room where more valuable considerations were disposed of under the Speaker's hammer than in any other place on earth."

The bubble finally burst during the summer of 1872, in a scandal gigantic enough to match the stakes

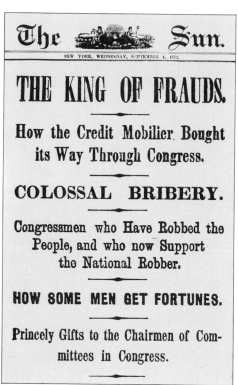

The Sun.

NEW YORK, WEDNESDAY, SEPTEMBER 4, 1872.

THE KING OF FRAUDS.

How the Credit Mobilier Bought its Way Through Congress.

COLOSSAL BRIBERY.

Congressmen who Have Robbed the People, and who now Support the National Robber.

HOW SOME MEN GET FORTUNES.

Princely Gifts to the Chairmen of Committees in Congress.

the railroad barons had played for. The furor exploded out of a personal conflict between Oakes Ames and Thomas Durant at the Union Pacific. Ames always insisted that he had been deputized by the martyred Lincoln to take the U.P.'s finances under control. And he insisted that honest patriotism, as much as entrepreneurial zeal, spurred him to do just that. "Save the credit of the road!" he announced, and he put the credit of his shovel company on the line to do so. But Durant, a scoundrel first and a patriot last, wanted nothing but riches. A bitter duel broke out between Ames's Boston money and the New York money represented by Thomas Durant. Ames ousted the Doctor from control of the Credit Mobilier. Durant fought back hard, and the scandal spilled out of the U.P.'s closet into the courts.

The ensuing publicity forced Congress to investigate the Credit Mobilier, and the firm's shady dealings were laid bare. Letters from Ames to his colleagues, read into the record, showed that he had distributed Credit Mobilier stock among his fellow Congressmen, virtually free; they could pay for the shares out of future dividends, which were enormous. Ames had made no bones about his reason for doing this. "We want more friends in this Congress," he wrote at one point. He dryly added: "I have found there is no difficulty about getting men to look after their own property."

The scandal grew to implicate Schuyler Colfax, Vice President of the United States, and rumors of bribery extended to a future Presidential candidate (James G. Blaine), a future President (James A. Garfield) and President Ulysses S. Grant himself. The scandal also aroused all of the public's accumulated wrath at corrupt officialdom, fast-buck profiteering, the full spectrum of shoddy ethics and unscrupulous behavior that had colored the nation's business since the Civil War.

But the greatest scorn was reserved for the unfortunate Oakes Ames. He sat in one witness chair after another for more than a year, while two separate Con-

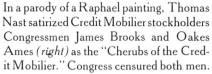

In a parody of a Raphael painting, Thomas Nast satirized Credit Mobilier stockholders Congressmen James Brooks and Oakes Ames (*right*) as the "Cherubs of the Credit Mobilier." Congress censured both men.

gressional committees came to a single conclusion: of $73 million poured into the Union Pacific, no more than $50 million could be justified as true costs. Through most of that ordeal, Ames's pride in having fulfilled the mandate given him by Abraham Lincoln seemed to fog his understanding of what the fuss was about. "I have risked reputation, fortune, everything," he testified, with complete conviction. "I have kept to the truth through good and evil report, denying nothing, concealing nothing, reserving nothing. Who will say that I alone am to be offered up as a sacrifice to appease a public clamor or expiate the sins of others?" But a sacrifice was needed, and Ames suffered the disgrace of a vote of censure passed overwhelmingly by Congress. He went home to Massachusetts a broken man; a few months after his return he was dead of a stroke.

His old rival and partner in crime came to a different end. Thomas Durant was often mentioned but seldom seen during the investigations. The Doctor was living quietly in the Catskills at the time; he had sold his in-

terest in the railroad itself years before, and he vanished into the cluster of millionaires who walked safely away from the Union Pacific. Though he built one more railroad — a tiny stretch in New York State — and played with a grandiose scheme for a U.S.-Canada line, his remaining years were spent in pleasant retirement.

Everybody walked away safely from the Central Pacific. In July of 1873 banner headlines in the New York *Sun* turned the nation's attention to the business practices of the Big Four:

THE ACME OF FRAUD

THE CREDIT MOBILIER OUTDONE

THE CENTRAL PACIFIC RING

$211,299,328.17 GOBBLED!

Like Ames before him, Collis Huntington was called to testify before a Congressional investigating committee, but the canny Sacramento wheeler-dealer handled himself more skillfully. He couldn't be very helpful,

Grant's Vice President, Schuyler Colfax,
with family and friends, enjoys a railroad
outing to Utah in 1869. His interest in
the Union Pacific was warm and personal:
he already owned Credit Mobilier stock.

he said. An unfortunate fire had gutted his company's headquarters and destroyed all its books a month or so earlier — he could speak only from memory.

Huntington's memory proved curiously spotty and unreliable. Along with a stream of offhand "I don't remember's," the mastermind of the C.P. displayed an astonishing inability to explain the workings of his own railroad. Nonetheless, Congress concluded that, through their Contract & Finance Company, the Big Four had pocketed at least $63 million; in addition, they held most of the C.P. capital stock, valued at $100 million, and controlled nine million acres of land granted to them by the government. But no crime was proved and no indictments were brought; the disheartened committee did not even call upon Stanford, Hopkins and Crocker to testify. So the Big Four were hardly grazed during the crash of reputations around them, and destiny treated them kindly all the rest of their lives.

That kind of good luck was in limited supply. Two months after the Central Pacific scandal became public, a new furor arose over the affairs of the Northern Pacific Railroad. The line had begun as the idealistic vision of one Josiah Perham *(page 214)*, a lecturer and impresario from Boston who made a living by displaying a painted panorama of the Great Lakes country. That attraction proved so popular that Perham began arranging low-cost excursion trains to the region. The success of this venture inspired him to conceive the magnificently named Perham's People's Pacific Railroad, which was, he proclaimed, "to be owned by the people in small sums." Congress liked the preposterous idea well enough to give Josiah Perham 47 million acres of land and a charter. But Perham was no railroad baron, and his line went broke. In 1869 it had fallen into the hands of New York financier Jay Cooke at a cost of 15 cents a share.

Cooke ran the gamut of railroad-baron shenanigans: a fraudulent construction company, the bribing of Congressmen, and the rest. (Along with the ever-reliable Schuyler Colfax and President-to-be Rutherford B. Hayes, the recipients of Cooke's benefactions included Ulysses Grant, whose funds for his 1872 reelection

> **Oh, My Country !**
> The following is in pencil on the Ames letter:
> Oakes Ames's list of names, as shown to-day to me for Credit Mobilier, is: *Shares.*
> BLAINE of Maine - - - 3,000
> PATTERSON of New Hampshire 3,000
> WILSON, Massachusetts - - 2,000
> PAINTER (Rep.) for Quigley - 3,000
> S. COLFAX, Speaker - - - 2,000
> SCOFIELD and KELLEY, Pa. 2,000 each.
> ELIOT, Massachusetts - - 3,000
> DAWES, Massachusetts - - 2,000
> FOWLER, Tennessee - - 2,000
> BOUTWELL, Massachusetts - 2,000
> BINGHAM and GARFIELD, O. 2,000 each.
> Endorsed: Oakes Ames, Jan. 30, 1868.

campaign were swelled by several million from Cooke's coffers.) Then, in 1873, a financial bloc led by the New York banking house of J. P. Morgan and Company set out to destroy Cooke's empire. Just as Cooke was in the act of swinging a $300 million government loan to assist his unfinished railroad, his enemies closed in upon him. Spreading the rumor that Cooke's credit had become well-nigh worthless, they blocked the government loan. Cooke's railroad operations ground to a halt; soon afterward, his bank closed its doors.

The fall of Cooke and Company proved to be a disaster for the nation as well. It was the key link in a chain of events that led to a financial panic in 1873 and the longest and worst depression the United States had ever known up to that time. Beginning with a stock-market crash on Black Friday, September 19, the depression paralyzed the country for five years. It was a long, difficult season for Western railroad enthusiasts, who felt seduced and abandoned.

The temporary disillusion of the West was based upon painful facts and ugly truths. But an overriding judgment was expressed by Charles Francis Adams Jr., a grandson of John Quincy Adams and a future president of the Union Pacific. Adams had been one of the first to point out the iniquities of the Huntington-Durant school of railroading, in which, as he said, "every expedient which the mind of man can devise has been brought into play to secure to the capitalist the largest possible profit with the least possible risk." But he also saw that the squalid details of the railroads' birth could not detract from the great fact of their presence. Even while the barons stole, "the locomotive was at work, and all the obstructions which they placed in its way could at most only check but never overcome the impetus it had given to material progress."

Adams' conclusion, reached after weighing all the evidence, was just and stirring: "The simple truth was that through its energetic railroad development, the country was producing real wealth as no country ever produced it before. Behind all the artificial inflation which so clearly foreshadowed a catastrophe, there was also going on a production that exceeded all experience."

A Union Pacific crew in Nebraska lays rails during early stages of construction. Idlers are U.P. guests.

3 | Working on the railroad

When the persuading and the planning for the Western railroads had finally been completed, the really challenging task remained: the dangerous, sweaty, backbreaking, brawling business of actually building the lines. The men who took it on comprised the most cosmopolitan work crew in American history. They included Civil War veterans and freed slaves, Irish and German immigrants, Mormons and atheists, Shoshonis, Paiutes, Washos and wiry little Chinese who drank boiled tea instead of doubtful water and who brought along (and also paid) their own cooks.

At the peak of their labors the work crews laid two to five miles of track a day. The men filled ravines, ran spidery trestles across rivers and valleys and punched holes through mountains. And they did all these jobs largely by their own muscle power.

Flatcars carried rails to within half a mile of the railhead; there the iron was loaded onto carts. An eyewitness described the procedure: "A light car, drawn by a single horse, gallops up to the front with its load of rails. Two men seize the end of a rail and start forward, the rest of the gang taking hold by twos until it is clear of the car. They come forward at a run. At the word of command, the rail is dropped in its place, right side up. Less than 30 seconds to a rail for each gang, and so four rails go down to the minute."

As the pictures on these pages show, the building of the railroad was a sight indeed. And when that job, too, was done, the driving of the final spike (*pages 120-123*) set off a jubilee the like of which America had seldom seen.

Three-deck rolling bunkhouses were home for the laborers who extended the St. Paul, Minneapolis & Manitoba — later the Great Northern — from Minot in the Dakotas to Helena, Montana Territory. Guarded by soldiers who took their band along, the men laid 643 miles of track between April 2 and November 19, 1887, a record that still stands.

Pushing the Central Pacific across Sailor's Spur, a ravine in the High Sierra, Chinese crews hack at the mountain by hand, while horses pulling dumpcarts haul off earth and rock in thousands of tiny loads to fill the defile. As winter snows approached, some crews put in three-shift, 24-hour days.

On a rickety temporary trestle in the Cascade mountains, a Northern Pacific crew lines up proudly with visiting wives and children. The grade in the Cascades sometimes measured a relatively steep 5.6 per cent, yet many train crews resented the route's replacement by a tunnel, since the old road traversed some of the Northwest's finest scenery.

0177

Blank No. 1.

THE WESTERN UNION TELEGRAPH COMPANY.

The rules of this Company require that all messages received for transmission, shall be written on the message blanks of the Company, under and subject to the conditions printed thereon, which conditions have been agreed to by the sender of the following message.

THOS. T. ECKERT, Gen'l Sup't, NEW YORK. | 11 50 pm | WILLIAM ORTON, Pres't, O. H. PALMER, Sec'y, NEW YORK.

117

Dated Promontory Utah via Omaha 9 186

Received at May 9

To Oliver Ames

Prest.

You can make affidavit of completion of road to Promontory Summit.

G. M. Dodge

Ch[ie]f Engr

11.400 Coll

Rec^d May 10

"A grand anvil chorus across the plains"

Once the routes were settled and the financing had been arranged, a new breed of railroader appeared on the scene to translate the grandiose paper schemes into mile upon mile of solid roadbed and track. Tough-minded contractors, subcontractors, engineers and gang foremen — many of them fresh out of the Union Army — went West when the war was over, rolled up their sleeves and built railroads.

During the three decades that followed Appomattox, this dogged cadre drove and cajoled an amorphous, polyglot work force numbering in the tens of thousands in one of the most ambitious enterprises of the 19th Century. Basically they laid track. But what they truly created was a new social order, turning a wilderness into a potential home for any farmer, journeyman, doctor, lawyer, tradesman or bank clerk who could scrape up the price (eight cents a mile) of a ticket west.

Well before century's end, these resolute, muscular crews completed not one but five separate transcontinental rail links. After the historic joining of the Union Pacific and the Central Pacific rails at Promontory Summit on May 10, 1869 — as announced in the laconic telegram shown at left — came the completion of the Southern Pacific (1883), the Northern Pacific (1883), the Atchison, Topeka and Santa Fe (1885) and the Great Northern (1893). The crews plotted the grades and curves, molded the roadbeds, built the bridges and tunnels to support, by 1890, a total of more than 70,000 miles of track between the Mississippi River and the Pacific Ocean. Compared to the

3,200 jumbled, short-line track miles in the West in 1865, the accomplishment was astounding.

Blizzards in the Sierra, Wasatch and Rocky mountains confronted crews with 40-foot drifts. Avalanches buried men alive. Homemade nitroglycerin blew them to smithereens. Sioux and Cheyennes scalped them. Temporary tracks laid over frozen rivers vanished in spring thaws. Floods washed out roadbeds by the mile. Brickbat and dynamite wars raged between the work gangs of rival roads.

Still they drove on. Five men to the 500-pound rail, 28 or 30 spikes to the rail, three blows to the spike, two pairs of rails to the minute, 400 rails to the mile — and half a continent to go. "A grand Anvil Chorus [is] playing across the plains . . . 21 million [strokes and] this great work of modern America is complete," an Eastern newspaper reporter crowed in 1868 from the end of the Union Pacific track as it pushed westward toward the Great Salt Lake.

Perhaps only a journalist, viewing such a chaotic enterprise in mid-stride, would be inspired to liken it to an anvil chorus. An American marvel, however, it incontestably was — though that feature hardly was assured at the outset. When construction began, the first Western railroads off the mark — the Union Pacific pushing west out of Omaha and the Central Pacific pushing east from Sacramento — were lacking in just about everything. Their greatest shortage was the commodity they needed most — labor, at both ends of the project and at both ends of the organization chart. Men who had gone West to get rich quick scorned pick-and-shovel work unless it was on their own gold or silver claim. Not until the Civil War had been over for a year or more did this situation somewhat improve. By 1866 a shrinking peacetime economy began to put a financial pinch on veterans from both sides of the Mason-Dixon Line and increasing numbers of day laborers were glad

In a deadpan, 11-word wire, Grenville M. Dodge told Union Pacific president, Oliver Ames, that the greatest industrial enterprise of its day was completed. The rails had met at Promontory, Utah, and the affidavit would release U.S. subsidies to the U.P.

In June 1864, upon the official opening of its first 31 miles of track, the Central Pacific published a timetable. Chugging along a five-station route, Central Pacific trains earned over $47,000 by the year's end.

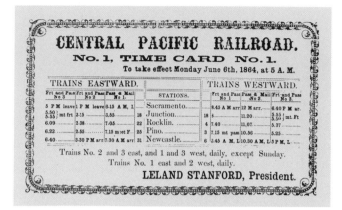

CENTRAL PACIFIC RAILROAD.

No. 1, TIME CARD No. 1.

To take effect Monday June 6th, 1864, at 5 A. M.

TRAINS EASTWARD.				STATIONS.		TRAINS WESTWARD.		
Frt and Pass No 3	Frt and Pass No 2	Pass & Mail No. 1				Frt and Pass No 1	Pass & Mail No 2	Frt and Pass No 3
5 P M leave	1 P M leave	6.15 A M, l.		Sacramento		8.45 A M arr	12 M arr.	6.40 P M ar.
5.50 } mt frt 5.55	2.15	6.55	18	Junction	18	8	11.20	5.55 } mt. Ft 5.50
6.09	2.38	7.05	22	Rocklin	4	7.40	11.07	5.37
6.22	2.55	7.15 m } et F.	25	Pino	3	7.15 mt pass	10.56	5.25
6.40	3.30 P M arr	7.30 A M arr	31	Newcastle	6	6.45 A M, L	10.30 A M, L	5 P M, L

Trains No. 2 and 3 east, and 1 and 3 west, daily, except Sunday.
Trains No. 1 east and 2 west, daily.

LELAND STANFORD, President.

to take work where they could find it. Moreover, many ex-Army officers were discovering that the railroads offered the best outlets for their particular skills.

Among the latter was Grenville Dodge, who, having had enough of Indian-fighting by 1866, decided to return to the railroad. In May 1866, he took command as chief engineer of the Union Pacific.

On the other side of the Great Divide — on the west slope of the Sierra, in fact — the Central Pacific had begun at last to feel the effects of an equally forceful hand on the helm. Charlie Crocker of the Big Four had been outlandishly miscast as a purveyor of yard goods. But he found himself in his element as the profane, bull-headed boss contractor of all C.P. construction.

Filling out the organization charts between the Crockers and the Dodges at the top and the pick-and-shovel men and the rust eaters (as the men who handled the rails were known to call themselves) at the bottom were other men of special talents and dispositions. They were the surveyors, working hundreds of miles out in the boondocks with their support teams of transitmen and chainmen, staking down a path through Indian country; they were the boss graders devising ways to slice the side off a granite mountain and use the junk to fill a canyon next to it; they were the engineers who, when they could not wait for a tunnel to be bored, ramrodded temporary track over the mountain and kept right on going; and they were the hundreds of other skilled, inventive and forceful men who took robust pleasure in hard work and the doing of tasks that had never been done before.

On the Central Pacific the man all hands learned to regard with awe — and ultimately with terror — was James

Harvey Strobridge, Crocker's chief of staff. A gangling six-foot-plus New Englander who had learned railroad-building as a young man among the hills of Vermont, Strobridge, now 37, could see no reason to regard the Sierra with greater respect. He was a slave driver fortified with a spectacular fund of profanity and a merciless conviction that the men he drove — ultimately 10,000 at a time — were "about as near brutes as they can get." Strobridge lost his right eye while impatiently monitoring a laggard black-powder blast. He took to wearing a patch over the empty socket and the Chinese roustabouts, who had acquired a modicum of pidgin English, marked him down, in fear, as "One Eye Bossy Man." Once, setting forth his labor relations policy with dry understatement, Strobridge remarked, "Men generally earn their money when they work for me."

In vivid contrast to Strobridge stood Brigadier General John Stephen Casement, an Ohioan who topped out at five feet four inches. Despite his full beard, Casement and his younger brother, Dan, who was even shorter at "five-foot-nothing," looked, according to a contemporary, like "twelve-year-old boys, but requiring larger hats." Diminutive the general was, but as a commander of men he turned out to be 10 feet tall.

General Casement signed a contract with U.P. director Dr. Thomas Durant to lay track in return for $750 per mile. His technique, every bit as effective as Strobridge's, was founded in loyalty rather than fear. He took the raw material he could get — Irish immigrants fleeing famine at home, discharged Union and Confederate soldiers, fed-up farmers and disillusioned prospectors, drifters, drunks, even a few Indian women. These he drilled relentlessly into a quasi-military army that could not only spike down track with the speed and precision of a close-order drill team but was just as ready to repel Indian raiders with the Spencer rifles stocked in the work train.

Although Strobridge and Casement were contemporaries and eventually would become rivals, their positions with the railroads they worked for were not analogous. Strobridge was overall construction boss, but he reported to Crocker. Casement was his own boss, working for the U.P. on contract. Yet, in the final race to close the transcontinental rail gap, the two found themselves pitted against one another in one of the most exciting contests the world has ever known. At

the beginning, however, their track-laying was undertaken at such a great distance from each other, and their immediate challenges were so different, that they might have been boxers facing off in separate rings.

Strobridge and the eastward-stretching Central Pacific, being only 70 miles from the granite crest of the Sierra, got to the heavy going far sooner than did their colleague-enemies of the Union Pacific, who were starting west from the flatlands, 680 miles from the Rockies. The C.P. tracks were a mere 34 miles out of Sacramento when, to maintain grade, it became necessary to slice out the Bloomer Cut, an 800-foot-long trench, 63 feet deep, through a mound of aggregate nearly as dense as granite. The C.P. men began using black powder on the cut. They worked across the crest of the obstruction, blasting out one shallow cavity, cleaning up, then blasting again and again.

Getting enough black powder had always been a problem and the shortages were aggravated by the demands of the Civil War and the uncertainties of transportation around the Horn or across the Isthmus of Panama. Once, when Strobridge was in a hurry for 5,000 kegs of the stuff, Secretary of War Edwin Stanton, who held all railroad contractors in bitter contempt, testily turned down the request. So Collis Huntington, calling the Secretary "a hog and no gentleman," went over his head to the President. Lincoln, knowing nothing of the quarrel, decided that the requisition "seems proper to me. Yes, that is very proper." So he signed the order.

Raising the army of human muscle to move the mountains out of the way was, for many months, a conundrum even more perplexing. While Crocker advertised throughout California for 5,000 men, grandly offering "permanent" employment, he was seldom able to sign on more than 800. Meanwhile, every payday the C.P. lost upward of 100 to the more attractive lures of the fleshpots or the Nevada mines.

As early as 1865, however, Crocker found the solution to the problem, albeit against Strobridge's will.

Crocker had repeatedly urged his construction boss to try out the Chinese — who had come to California a decade earlier to rework the tailings of the gold mines left by the forty-niners — but Strobridge was dead set against the idea. Strobridge possessed more than his full share of the white man's contempt for Celestials, as he and his fellow Californians called these strange little men with their dishpan straw hats, pigtails and floppy blue pajamas. He measured them against his brawny Irish crews (the Terrestrials) and concluded that the Chinese were too frail for the work and too unmechanical to perform it. Besides, Strobridge argued, who could ever feed them the outlandish fodder they ate? Cuttlefish, bamboo shoots, mushrooms, rice, even seaweed — hardly food fit for railroad builders.

But when a crew of Irishmen threatened to strike, Strobridge, desperate, reluctantly agreed to take on 50 Orientals as an experiment. The ploy was doubly successful: not only did it send the Irish scurrying back to the railhead, but the Chinese worked wonders. Strobridge soon signed on another gang of 50, then another and another until, to his dismay, he learned that Crocker had nearly emptied the Chinatowns of Sacramento and San Francisco of able-bodied men, ignoring only the rich merchants and lords of the tongs.

By mid-March, 1865, Crocker was forced to turn to professional labor contractors, who recruited Chinese farm boys from the Cantonese districts of Sinong and Sinwai. The usual method was for these agents to advance passage money — $40 by steamship and $25 to $35 by sailing vessel — to be repaid, with interest often as high as five per cent per month, out of the man's salary after he started drawing his pay. But before being shipped to Sacramento to begin work on the track, the

A band of scalp-seeking Cheyenne Indians charges a crew of Kansas Pacific graders in Kansas during the summer of 1867. For a time, in

bewildered young Orientals were formed into small gangs of 12 to 20 men, each with its own cook and headman. The latter was a Chinese who had been in California for some time. While he worked along with the rest, he also acted as interpreter and clerk, collecting wages for the rest, deducting monthly assessments for food and the labor contractors.

Strobridge had learned quickly that the scrawny little bodies of his Chinese workers — running to not more than 110 pounds — husbanded amazing reserves of sinewy strength and endurance. Moreover, the Celestials were quick to learn, slow to complain and ready to start work when the whistle blew. They did bicker shrilly among themselves, and there was occasional bloodshed between men from Sinong and Sinwai; and they did gamble incessantly. But, unlike the volatile Irish, the Chinese were not inclined to strike, did not get drunk on payday, did not frequent whorehouses in the mining towns along the C.P. right of way and did not lean on the pick handle when the boss was not looking. They did have an outrageous habit of bathing every day and they did drink enormous quantities of boiled tea — which did not make them sick the way carelessly quaffed ditchwater frequently afflicted white laborers.

Soon Strobridge had occasion to learn that his Chinese — by this time known as "Crocker's pets" — were as courageous as they were reliable. The circumstance arose when — 57 miles out from Sacramento — they confronted a shale mass, aggressively shoved out from the flank of the Sierra. Standing 2,000 feet above the gorge of the American River, to which it descended at an angle of $75°$, Cape Horn (as the rocky spur soon came to be known) seemed to forbid all passage. And yet this was where the surveyors had decided that the rails

response to such attacks, the railroad maintained a full stock of guns in its supply trains and called upon the U.S. Army for protection.

Fresh from a supper served in a triple-decker bunkhouse-on-wheels, workers on the St. Paul, Minneapolis & Manitoba Railroad gather at trackside for a photographer. The front row includes a group of friendly Indian visitors, and one of the railroad men holds a papoose in his arms.

came to life one morning in the fall of '67. U.P. track at the time had reached Antelope, between Julesburg and Cheyenne. "It is half past five and time for the hands to be waked up," the reporter noted. "This is done by ringing a bell on the sleeping car until everyone turns out and by giving the fellows under the car a smart kick and by pelting the fellows in the tents on the top with bits of clay. In a very few minutes they are all out stretching and yawning. Another bell and they crowd in for breakfast. The table is lighted by hanging lamps, for it is yet hardly daylight. At intervals of about a yard are wooden buckets of coffee, great plates of bread and platters of meat. There is no ceremony: every man dips his cup into the buckets of coffee and sticks his own fork into whatever is nearest him. If a man has got enough and is through, he quietly puts one foot on the middle of the table and steps across." With breakfast finished, the crews set to work at 6:30. They usually stayed on the job to sundown, with an hour off at noon for lunch.

The actual laying of the tracks by Casement's crew was a ballet of muscle and iron (pages 82-83). It began when lightweight carts, each drawn by a horse along the newest section of track, were positioned beside a stockpile containing all the supplies the track gang would need for the coming day. Six-man crews hastily piled each of the little carts with 16 rails plus the proper number of spikes, bolts and rail couplings called fishplates. Then, in series, the carts would be hauled by running horses to the very end of the last pair of rails spiked down.

The bed of each cart was equipped with rollers, and the rails were removed faster than they had left the flat-car. They were pulled off in pairs, five men to a rail. Now came the men with the notched wooden gauge, spacing each pair of rails precisely four feet eight and one half inches apart — and the spike men would begin swinging their mauls. Meanwhile the cart would have been unceremoniously dumped off the tracks to make way for the next one coming up on the run. Then back it would go for a new burden of rails.

As they advanced, the U.P. tracks created towns —and then, by moving on, abolished most of them. Every 60 miles or so along the right of way a semi-permanent metropolis would arise. The first edifice would be the "Big Tent" wherein a tired man could slake his thirst, or any other lust he might still be capable of summoning up after a day on the ties.

The U.P. camp followers were fast-dollar types —gamblers, saloonkeepers, con men, pimps and whores. "These women," wrote the New York *Tribune's* prim Henry M. Stanley—who had not yet discovered Dr. Livingston in Darkest Africa—"are expensive articles, and come in for a large share of the money wasted. In broad daylight they may be seen gliding through the dusty streets carrying fancy derringers slung to their waists, with which tools they are dangerously expert. Western chivalry will not allow them to be abused by any man they may have robbed. Mostly everyone seemed bent on debauchery and dissipation."

These makeshift towns—North Platte, Julesburg, Cheyenne, Laramie, Corinne—gave birth to the phrase "hell on wheels." From Julesburg, boss Sam Reed wrote to his wife: "Vice and crime stalk unblushingly in the mid-day sun." In short, the U.P. rust eaters were offered every convenience for swiftly unburdening themselves of some of the hardest dollars ever earned—$35 a month for a semiskilled Irishman—about the same as their wheelbarrow-pushing Chinese counterparts were getting out West. But pay for white workers on both lines included free bed and board, while the Chinese housed themselves in tents and dugouts and paid for their own exotic chow, shipped to them via San Francisco's Chinatown.

Social life along the Central Pacific right of way was completely different. Strobridge would not tolerate the temptations of the U.P.'s hells on wheels. The Chinese had never given him that sort of trouble, except in the one instance when he had caught 40 of them smoking opium in an impoverished den—a form of relaxation which he ended by confiscating pipes and drug and by personally beating up the organizers. But he still had some Irish working for him and they still cherished the privilege of a payday spree.

At first they could let off steam in the Sierra mining towns. But later, when the C.P. reached the Nevada desert where there were no towns, Strobridge was able to block the vice peddlers because the only available water was that carried in his tank cars. Good morals were not his basic concern, good business was. And man-hours were too precious to be wasted in fleshpots and their probable aftermath. Strobridge discouraged

booze merchants intrepid enough to make the trip to the end of track by charging them more to water their horses than they could get from their sales of whiskey. If this did not work, Strobridge simply gathered up a few burly track hands, took the law in his own fists, and smashed what offended him.

However, man-made pitfalls were easier to guard against than some that nature devised. Among the most unpredictable were the famous summer Platte River storms, which pounced with shattering violence upon U.P. crews out on the open prairie. One such storm was observed by photographer William Henry Jackson, who was later to compile a magnificent photographic gallery of the American West.

"It came down raging and howling like a madman," Jackson wrote. "It rocked and shook us and started some of the wagons on their wheels. We had serious apprehensions that we should be capsized. The rain came down in steady torrents—the roaring thunder and the flashing lightning were incessant, reverberating through the heavens with an awful majesty. The rain came right through the wagon sheets, but we hauled a buffalo robe over our heads."

Summers were bad enough but the winters at the working ends of the two lines were worse. The winter of 1866-1867 was talked about for years by crews who lived through it. On the open prairie it halted U.P. operations altogether. But while snowbound trackmen helled away the winter in the stews of North Platte, January handed the supply crews a boon by freezing the Missouri 16 inches thick at Omaha.

That was enough to bear the weight of a locomotive; Jack Casement laid temporary rails across the ice so that, for the first time, it became possible to stockpile large supplies of material on the west bank, material that would not have to be ferried past the river's bars and snags and through the current that made river transport particularly perilous. But the time gained was more than wiped out when the spring thaw sent the snow-melt from the mountains raging down upon the Plains. Although the long bridge at the Loup River held against the torrents, the flood tore away a mile of embankment and track at both ends of the bridge, scattering ties and bending rails into hairpins.

Disastrous as the season had been for the U.P., the winter of '66 was even worse for the C.P. It caught

A temporary trestle, 1,100 feet long by 130 feet high, spans May Creek in western Washington with a maze of wood beams and iron bolts. One newspaper reported such bridges would "shake the nerves of the stoutest hearts when they see what is expected to uphold a train in motion."

Pecking away with hand drills, Northern Pacific workmen carve the nearly two-mile-long Stampede Tunnel in the Cascades. Sometimes the job advanced only inches per day; completion took about two years.

Strobridge's crews at their highest, most exposed and most vulnerable point of work in the Sierra. Some 38 miles above Dutch Flat, Crocker's pets — the C.P. employed upwards of 6,000 Chinese by now — were in their first full winter of boring the Summit Tunnel, the last, longest and highest of the six bores needed to get up and through the Sierra before the line reached the long, steep pitch down the eastern slope of the range. At the same time crews were already at work night and day on the nine tunnels that would be needed to make the descent to the deserts of Nevada.

Summit Tunnel would have been a brute in the best of weather. A bore 20 feet high had to be punched through 1,659 feet of solid granite, 7,032 feet above sea level and 124 feet below the rugged summit of Donner Pass. But then the blizzards came. That savage winter of 1866-1867 counted 44 of them. One storm lasted 13 days with no letup, dumping six feet of snow in the first four days, a 10-foot accumulation by the time the storm subsided at last. The previous winter, which had provided ample evidence of the amounts of snow that could be expected in the Sierra, had persuaded the C.P. to build its first snowplow, a behemoth 30 feet long, with a front end styled like the prow of a battleship, and weighted to keep it on the track as it pushed the heavy snow aside.

It was not enough; up to 12 locomotives could not push the plow through the drifts. Blasting powder and food had to be dragged laboriously on horse-drawn sledges from Dutch Flat to the isolated tunnelers. When conditions became entirely impassable, isolated work crews were cut off for weeks at a time, existing on emergency stocks of food.

But short rations were only one storm hazard. Winds raging in from the Pacific built fantastic snow cornices on the Sierra ridges. When these broke loose, avalanches came tearing down on roads and camps.

In one such slide 20 Chinese died when their insubstantial barracks were uprooted and carried bodily down the mountain. And nobody ever kept an accurate census of the Celestials who vanished by ones, twos or threes under lesser avalanches.

In places the cuts and canyons were drifted 60 feet deep, but the Chinese slugged on; with Strobridge hounding them, there was nothing else they could do. They lived and worked literally under the snow. They had to cut passageways between their log barracks and the tunnel entrance in order to continue to hack at the harder granite inside the mountain.

The going inside was difficult indeed. Crews labored around the clock. But even with unlimited quantities of blasting powder — the stuff was now being manufactured in California mills and Crocker was sending Strobridge as many as 500 kegs a day — progress was a mere eight inches each 24 hours. What took time was boring drill holes. Not only did the mountain resist, blunting and breaking the hand-held iron drills, but the holes themselves, in order to accept an effective charge, had to be pounded wider and far deeper than in softer rock. Otherwise the explosion simply would blow back out of the hole as if from the mouth of a cannon.

The year before, Strobridge had experimented with the newfangled European invention, nitroglycerin, eight times as powerful as black powder and therefore needing far smaller holes. But an incident that spring had made it impossible for him to procure more "blasting oil." On April 16th, at precisely 13.5 minutes past 1 p.m., San Franciscans were treated to a precursor of the famous quake, when a violent explosion shook the city. The blast, which killed 12 bystanders and sent a bloody arm flying through a third-story window, was traced to two crates of nitroglycerin that a Wells Fargo agent had unaccountably deposited in a back lot. Public reaction was so intense that virtually all shipment of the highly unstable stuff into California was suspended.

Snowed in and desperate for progress, Strobridge thought of a way to circumvent the ban. He hired a Scottish chemist named James Howden. Then he brought in separate shipments of glycerin and of nitric and sulphuric acids; these three ingredients of nitroglycerin were inert as long as they were kept apart. In a kitchen prepared for him at the summit of the majestic Sierra, like some satanic Merlin of the snows, the Scotsman set about cooking his hell's brew, a fresh batch every day to blow the guts out of the mountains.

Thereafter work in Summit Tunnel proceeded at twice the pace. By August the two headings met, and by November rail was laid through the Summit Tunnel. For the Central Pacific the going was progressively easier from there on.

But, far across the Great Basin, in the Platte River valley, the U.P. and General Dodge found themselves

A snowshed guards track in the Sierra
where drifts of over 40 feet had closed the
Central Pacific in winter. The road built
37 miles of sheds in 1868 and 1869,
using some 65 million board feet of timber.

As many as 12 engines were used to ram this Bucker snowplow through 30-foot Sierra drifts in the winter of 1867. In 1890 a rotary plow cleared as much track in an hour as the Bucker it replaced did in a day.

increasingly frustrated by a human impediment, the resentful Indian. The problem had never seriously affected the C.P. Charlie Crocker had made sure of that by issuing lifetime passes to Shoshoni, Cheyenne and other local chieftains permitting them to ride the passenger cars, and had also decreed that tribesmen of lesser rank might ride the freight cars free for 30 years.

Out on the Plains, however, U.P. construction crews found that the much fiercer Sioux and many Cheyennes were not to be bought off so cheaply.

Even before the Civil War had ended, General Dodge and his army units had been hard at work "pacifying" the Plains tribes with merciless vigor. After the war, General Philip Sheridan had ably taken up the job. Those Indians who would not peaceably submit to resettlement on a reservation were being systematically hunted down like vermin. Now the great gangs of railroad workers, following marks and flags left by the advance surveying parties, were pouring through western Nebraska and southeastern Wyoming, the traditional hunting grounds of the Sioux and the Cheyennes—and the Indians began to attack.

Given the degree of provocation and the vast, unguarded reaches the railroad covered, the wonder is that the Indians did not damage the line more. Perhaps it was not within the realm of their experience or imagination to wreak cold-blooded vengeance on such impersonal objects as steel rails and telegraph wires. They did attack trains to get at the people inside, and they tore down telegraph lines whose humming boded evil medicine; they even ripped up rails on occasion. But the Indians' strongest thrusts were made against the iso-

Racing to lay track—and obtain government loans—the Union Pacific and Central Pacific often built temporary wooden bridges like this U.P. trestle at Green River, Wyoming. When this photograph was made in 1868, a masonry replacement was already under construction (left).

109

lated groups of bridgebuilders, tie cutters and particularly the small advance parties of surveyors.

In their first direct encounters with the steam engine itself, the Indians were simply overwhelmed by a power beyond their conceiving. In 1866 a chief named Spotted Tail, leading a party of braves, came upon Jack Casement's crew laying track 150 miles west of Omaha. After a friendly demonstration of the warriors' skills with bow and arrow—to the genuine amazement of the track crew—the whites, not to be outdone, challenged the Indians to race their horses against the locomotive. Spotted Tail was persuaded to mount the engine cab to cheer his warriors on. With a hoot of the whistle and a war whoop from the braves, the event was underway. Showing good early foot, the Indians at first raced ahead but, as the iron horse gathered its sinews together, Spotted Tail found himself gazing disconsolately backward at his defeated brethren through the pall of smoke and ash billowing past the locomotive's stack.

One mounted war party of 50 or so warriors actually tried to capture a locomotive. Splitting their forces, they stretched rawhide lariats across the track and attached the ends to their saddles. When the train arrived and hit the rawhide barrier at 25 miles an hour, several of the Indians who were nearest the rails were swung along with their ponies into the pounding drive wheels and dismembered.

It can be imagined how much amusement that story afforded the idlers in the jerkwater stations west of Omaha. But when the Indians succeeded in wrecking a train, which they did occasionally, it was spoken of in dark tones as a massacre. The incident at Plum Creek on August 6, 1867, was a prime example.

On that night a war party of Cheyennes traveling an ancient trail came upon the U.P. tracks. Moving north to escape an Army dragnet sweeping through southern Nebraska, the Cheyennes had their blood up. Led by a chief called Turkey Leg, they piled a barricade of loose ties on the track and lashed it there with telegraph wire ripped from the poles. Then they waited.

Back at Plum Creek when the wire went dead, the linesman on duty, a young Englishman named William Thompson, who wore his blond hair long, loaded five section hands, a spool of new wire, repair tools and six Spencer rifles aboard a hand-pump car and set out to find the break. In the darkness, they never saw the barricade, still less had a chance to unlimber their weapons. They hit the ties, went flying through the air and within seconds five of the six men were dead at the hands of the Cheyennes. Thompson himself staggered to his feet and was at once clubbed down. Before he could rise again he felt a searing pain circling his skull and knew that his scalp was being lifted.

Thompson saw his attacker striding away to join the others, carelessly tucking the long blond, bloody locks under his belt. Unnoticed by the Indian, the scalp fell and Thompson, thinking only that he had to repossess it, crawled to where it lay and crammed it in a pocket. Then, without any real hope, he began to creep away.

Meanwhile, with tools from the pump car and the spool of wire, the war party set about improving their ambush. They unbolted two rails, wrenched them up and with sheer massed muscle bent the rails back on themselves and lashed them with wire.

Unaware of what lay ahead, a night freight was pounding up from the east, its oil-fired headlight casting a feeble gleam ahead. Like Thompson, the engineer failed to see what waited for him until it was too late; the locomotive slid into the barricade with brakes screeching. The fireman was catapulted against the open firebox and died there; the engineer, impaled on the throttle lever, was hauled from his cab and killed.

Back at the end of the train, the rest of the crew leaped out of the caboose and managed to escape, running back toward Plum Creek. On the way, they succeeded in flagging down a following freight in time to prevent further tragedy. At the wreck, meanwhile, the Indians threw the corpses onto the burning locomotive and set about looting the train on which, to their immense satisfaction, they found a barrel of whiskey.

All the while, the half-conscious Thompson struggled toward Plum Creek, still clutching his scalp. He arrived there near dawn and a special train was called to take him to surgical help in Omaha, 250 miles to the east. Wrapped in sheets, he was placed in a boxcar where he lay clutching the handle of a bucket of water in which floated his scalp. In Omaha, he was treated by Dr. C. P. Moore, but the scalp, seven inches wide and nine inches from front to back, had been mauled too much and Dr. Moore did not try to sew it back on Thompson's head. The young Englishman survived and eventually went back to railroading. In grateful recog-

110

The big shoot-out for the Leadville line

Westward-stretching railroads sometimes fought each other even harder than they battled avalanches, Indians or deserts. In such skirmishes tough men at the top made for rough stuff in the field—like the four-year fracas between the Atchison, Topeka and Santa Fe and the competing Denver & Rio Grande.

In 1876 both lines were pushing south from Colorado into New Mexico, seeking freight markets. William J. Palmer, the Rio Grande's founder (*page 217*), started surveying a route through the mountains, but bold and bearded William B. Strong, the Santa Fe's general manager, beat him to it. A Santa Fe surveyor disguised as a sheepherder, complete with his sheep, had shadowed Palmer's surveyors. Early one morning in 1878 when Rio Grande men came to work, they found armed guards at strategic Raton Pass and Santa Fe men busy grading.

Palmer left the pass to Strong, but the following spring both roads lunged for the booming silver mines at Leadville, Colorado, where miners were hauling out up to 100,000 pounds of ore a day. This freight bonanza awaited the first railroad to reach Leadville, accessible only via the Grand Canyon of the Arkansas River, a notch 3,000 feet deep and in places barely wide enough to accommodate a single pair of rails.

Palmer and Strong each began laying track toward the canyon—and harassing each other's work crews with hired guerrillas. The Santa Fe imported Dodge City's famous Bat Masterson, and scores of lesser *pistoleros*. The Rio Grande used local amateurs

William Palmer's forces hold a fort blocking Santa Fe crews in the Arkansas River canyon.

backed by sheriffs and state militia.

Saboteurs burned bridges, moved rival survey stakes and buried roadbeds under man-made avalanches. Rio Grande raiders swam the Arkansas, built a fort, ran off Santa Fe workers and threw their tools in the river. Riflemen behind hastily piled boulders sniped at work gangs.

The war so severely strained the Rio Grande's resources that Palmer's bondholders imposed a truce by forcing him to lease his road to the Santa Fe. Palmer promptly charged that Strong was deliberately ruining the Rio Grande by levying prohibitive freight rates on Rio Grande routes —and began plotting to retake his road, alerting vassals by telegraph.

Since both sides used the same wires and decoded each other's messages, Strong was forewarned. He garrisoned major Rio Grande stations, packing the Pueblo roundhouse with

riflemen under Masterson. In vain. Palmer's men simply swarmed aboard the Rio Grande's trains, booted off Strong's crews and steamed up and down the line, capturing stations as they went. At Cucharas, Palmer's Rio Grande forces killed two Santa Fe men and wounded two others. At Pueblo, Masterson and his men yielded the roundhouse—to assault by some accounts, to bribery by others.

The Rio Grande won that round but the war ended in a draw. Eastern financiers in 1880 dictated a compromise to stop the costly violence: the Rio Grande got Leadville; the Santa Fe, an exclusive route into New Mexico. Strong and Palmer, typical of their era, could have reached such a solution bloodlessly—but as Palmer remarked to his wife, "Amidst all the hot competition of this American business life there is a great temptation to be a little unscrupulous."

A worksheet for April 29, 1869, lists the names of the C.P. tracklayers who, on that day, lifted 1,000 tons of iron to lay a record 10 miles of track in 12 hours. For their feat, they were given four days' pay.

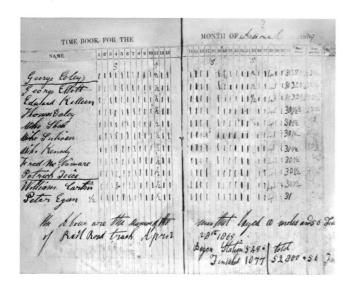

nition of his extraordinary recovery, Thompson had his scalp tanned and sent it to Dr. Moore as a gift.

As always, however, success for the Indian only hastened his end by hardening the will of the white man to take the continent. The more the Cheyennes and Sioux attacked the railroad, the more troops were sent to protect it. By 1868 some 5,000 soldiers were patrolling along and around the line of advance. With the threat of attack virtually gone, the last rein holding back the U.P. from a full gallop west was loosened.

An equal boost spurred on the C.P. Meeting the challenge of the climb up and over the Sierra had forged the Crocker-Strobridge team into a coolly efficient engineering and track-laying machine. A total of 15 tunnels had been needed to complete the momentous task. The prospect of continuing on over the relatively flat Nevada desert appeared simple by comparison. That the continent would be bridged could no longer be doubted. The only questions now were how speedily the deed could be finished and—most important—which company was going to get the farthest fastest and claim the most track.

An amendment to the Railroad Act of 1864 had permitted the Central Pacific to build beyond the eastern base of the Sierra, but no fixed meeting point had yet been decreed by competent federal authority. All through 1868 and into '69 both roads went bulling ahead on the tenable assumption that whoever laid the most rail was going to own the most railroad—and thus collect the greater amount of government bonds and land grants. The C.P. built 360 miles of track in '68 and the U.P. racked up 425.

Strobridge, down from the Sierra at last, drove his Chinese into the desert. But maddeningly, the Sierra winters were still proving to be the C.P.'s major obstacle. Although the track was completed across the mountains, the supplies—needed in ever-greater quantities as the pace of building increased—were bogged down in drifts and avalanches. When their snowplow had failed them in '67, Crocker, Montague and Strobridge had devised an effective solution—but it was taking time. The plan called for timber roofs to be built over the most frequently blocked stretches of track. The scheme worked, but the ponderous and costly ($2 million) covered sections, spanning in all 37 miles of track, would not be complete until months after the rails were joined at Promontory Summit.

Supplies or no supplies, Strobridge went fulminating through the Truckee Desert into the Humboldt Sink. Commenting on the speed of the operation, a junketing San Francisco newspaperman wrote: "I found it was no joke when General Crocker said it would be no easy task to overtake the end of the road. Taking out my watch, I timed the last half mile I saw laid, and it took a little less than 28 minutes."

Meanwhile, drumming along at top speed from the east, Dodge, Reed, Casement & Co. were, for the first time, coming up against the kind of terrain which had so long bedeviled Crocker and Strobridge in the west. But they had to dig only four tunnels compared to the 15 on the C.P. Three of the U.P. bores were needed to punch through the Wasatch Range in Utah. By far the most demanding of these was a 772-footer at the head of Echo Canyon.

They went at it, as they knew they ultimately had to. But in the race to outpace the C.P., they built a temporary looping bypass around Echo Summit, leaving the tunnel to be finished later.

Now the great grading race accelerated in earnest, each line operating on a theory that it could establish a sort of squatter's right to lay track later on by hurling miles of roadbed out ahead of the rails themselves. At one time, Samuel Reed had U.P. grading crews moving dirt and rocks 168 miles west of Ogden, Utah; coming the other way, S. S. Montague was working his C.P. graders across Utah, almost to the foot of Echo Sum-

mit, beneath which—sometime or other—the U.P. would have to complete its tunnel.

And at last the converging construction gangs—so long contestants at arms length—met in the great American desert. The nearly parallel advancing survey lines —one moving east, the other west—overlapped for some 200 miles. When the grading gangs met and went on to pass each other, they were so close that one crew would have to dodge the flying clods from the other's blasting charges, the timing of which both gangs neglected to announce before lighting their fuses.

The grading race at last roused the federal government to the necessity of stopping it. In January 1869, Secretary of Interior Orville H. Browning picked a commission of eminent civil engineers to go West and decide, once and for all, where the two grades would meet and the rails be joined.

The commission chose Promontory Summit, 56 miles west of Ogden; and the two railroads, amid threats, cajolery, back-room dealing and much grumbling, finally accepted.

The race was over. Grading, worth nothing in loans and land grants without rails on it, ceased forthwith. But sheer momentum kept the lines of track racing toward one another. On April 28, 1869, in fact, the Central Pacific's Chinese track gangs, working in harmony with the burly Irishmen who hauled the iron into place (page 112), spiked 10 miles and 56 feet of track in 12 hours in order to prove their superiority over the Union Pacific crews. It was a new record.

Now the gap was nearly closed. May 8th was set as the great day on which the rails should meet. The C.P.'s Leland Stanford arrived first on a special train loaded with West Coast dignitaries, railroad officials, newspapermen and assorted guests. He reached the rendezvous on schedule, in spite of a freak accident that might well have wiped out his entire party. A Chinese timber gang, felling trees in the Sierra, had sent a log

Steaming east past the Great Salt Lake, the Locomotive *Jupiter* draws Leland Stanford and a party of other dignitaries to the ceremonies marking the completion of the Central Pacific Railroad. At the same moment, one of the last of the wagon trains lumbers by, carrying settlers farther west.

The day the rails met

As the two locomotives from opposite ends of the West nosed toward one another in the desolate Utah landscape, not a man there—or on either ocean shore—doubted that this moment was among his nation's finest. In this year 1869 the continent was about to be bridged and, as more iron roads fanned out over the West, the United States, now truly one nation, soon would be a matchless power. So the linkup of the Central Pacific and the Union Pacific stirred the country as did no other industrial event of the century.

But the portentous moment proved more farcical than solemn. As Chinese workmen lifted the last rail to the roadbed, a photographer shouted to his assistant: "Shoot!" The Chinese dropped the rail and fled.

When they returned, C.P. President Leland Stanford swung at the final spike, ingeniously wired so that each blow would be telegraphed across the land. He missed. Nevertheless, the telegrapher flashed, "Dot. Dot. Dot. . . . Done." Guns boomed in Sacramento. San Franciscans danced in the streets and Mormons prayed in Salt Lake City.

Within the 30 years after 1869, four more transcontinental railroad lines clanged to completion; and eventually the emblems of the Western roads, emblazoned on engines and cars, became as familiar as postage stamps. The ceremony attendant on the driving of the final spikes reached a second peak with the linking of rails of the Northern Pacific *(pages 124-125)* in 1883. The road's president, Henry Villard, took four trainloads of friends to the scene. But by the time James Hill's Great Northern was finished in 1893, few people even noticed *(pages 126-127).*

Flanked by soldiers *(right),* workmen *(left)* and assorted dignitaries, the Union Pacific's *Engine 119 (foreground)* and the Central Pacific's *Jupiter* steam softly as all present await the driving of the final spike.

121

With the last rail laid at Promontory, the Central Pacific's *(left)* and Union Pacific's locomotives touch cowcatchers as two railroaders wield bottles of champagne, and Samuel S. Montague of the C.P. shakes hands with Grenville M. Dodge of the U.P. The C.P. later became the Southern Pacific and operated under the S.P. corporate symbol *(above)*.

Bareheaded, tycoon Henry Villard stands on one of four locomotives that hauled trainloads of celebrities to the completion ceremony for his Northern Pacific line at Gold Creek, Montana, on September 8, 1883. Former President U. S. Grant was among the guests, along with generals, bankers, legislators and a small army of newspapermen.

After a dank snowstorm in the Cascade mountains, two minor—and now forgotten—Great Northern officials drive a plain iron spike to complete the road on January 6, 1893. By that time the joining of rails had become so commonplace that James Hill, the Great Northern's gruff and crusty founder, did not bother to attend the impromptu ceremony.

126

4 The ride to California

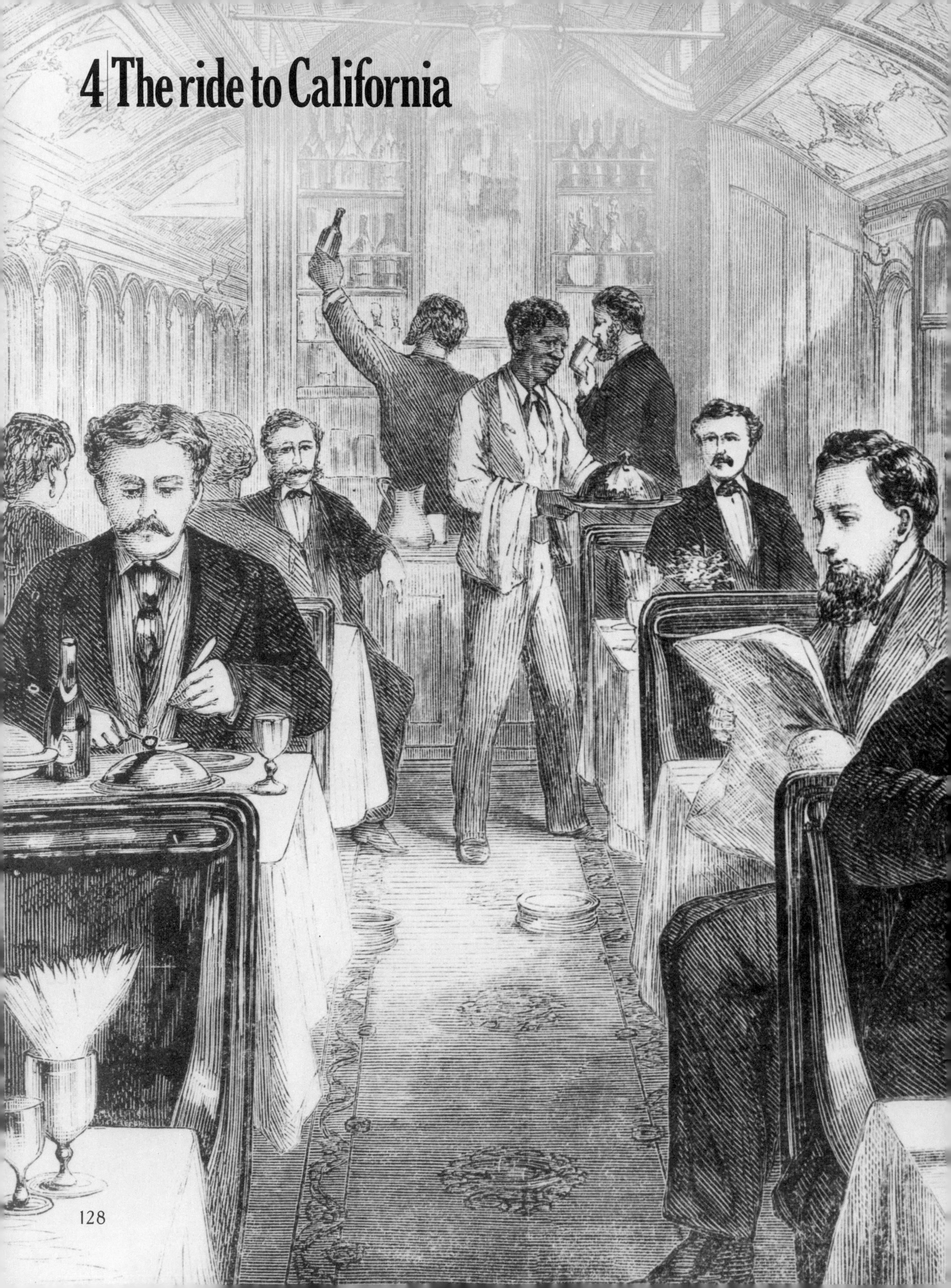

When the last spike had been driven to complete the Pacific line, every promise implicit in transcontinental railroading seemed about to come true. For the rich, the road offered splendid adventure — wining and dining at flower-decked tables *(left)*, relaxed sightseeing from observation cars and luxurious living aboard such trains as the eight-car *Pullman Hotel Express,* which boasted two libraries, a hair-dressing salon, two organs and, on one run, its own private newspaper, the *Transcontinental.* For the poor—emigrants from Eastern slums and new arrivals from Europe —the road held out quick, inexpensive transport to a new life out West.

To publicize these joys, the railroad companies rolled out heavy publicity campaigns, such as the stupendous promotional stunt launched in 1877 with Frank Leslie, a New York publisher. On July 7, Leslie embarked from New York on a five-month Western excursion designed to sell the public on the joys of riding the trains (and also of buying Mr. Leslie's newspaper). He took along writers, artists, his wife, his wife's dog and some friends.

For almost two years, *Frank Leslie's Illustrated Newspaper* presented readers with the wonders of the trip through engravings such as those shown on these pages. The accompanying text rhapsodized about dinners of oyster soup, antelope steak and quail, and over evenings of watching the moon glow on the snow of the Rockies. One of Leslie's women guests wrote: "The rarest and richest of all my journeying through life is this three-thousand miles by rail."

In an 1890 hotel car, passengers "may drink health and long life to friends at home," gushed Frank Leslie's newspaper, and dine on "steaks, chops, roasts, soups, pastry and all the good things of the table."

Late at night, trainmen bring a pair of new passengers to join cramped and weary coach riders. "It is a pathetic thing to see their nightly contrivances at comfort," *Leslie's* reported. But the newspaper's enthusiastic accounts of opportunities in the West helped to jam trains with travelers.

A blanketed and bemused Indian stands amid a group of singers aboard a Pullman parlor car of the *Pacific Hotel Express*. The organist was at times the train's conductor; to wangle the choice assignment to the Pacific run, a smart conductor might list organ playing as one of his talents.

Passengers rich, passengers poor

On May 15, 1869, five days after the joining of the rails at Promontory, the nation's first transcontinental railroad announced the inauguration of regular passenger service. Once a day westbound passengers would assemble at Omaha, Nebraska, and board the Pacific Express for Sacramento. And once a day from Sacramento the Atlantic Express would head east on a run of almost 2,000 miles to Omaha.

The moment had been so long in coming that some Americans could hardly believe it had arrived at last. *Frank Leslie's Illustrated Newspaper* spelled out the nature of the new era for its readers: "A journey over the plains was a formidable undertaking, that required great patience and endurance. Now all is changed. The shriek of the locomotive wakes the echoes of the slopes along the Sierras, through the cañons of the Wahsatch and the Black Hills, and his steady puffing is heard as he creeps along the mountain sides. The six months' journey is reduced to less than a week. The prairie schooner has passed away, and is replaced by the railway coach with all its modern comforts."

Comfort and speed—these were lures no traveler could resist. In 1870, the first full year of operations, nearly 150,000 passengers rode the line that stretched between Omaha and Sacramento; a dozen years later their number on that route alone soared to almost a million. And this huge traveling population came to form a microcosm of the West—of the men and women who lived there, or visited there, or merely passed through on their way to somewhere else.

At the top of the heap were the dudes and excursionists and just plain rich folk who rode first class.

With the exuberance of a circus poster, a Kansas Pacific advertisement of the late 1870s romanticizes Colorado's canyons, lakes, crags and streams to woo tourists.

In 1870, for a fare of $100 between Omaha and Sacramento, the railroad added a certain splendor to the comfort and speed of their journey. First-class passengers could ride in luxurious cars on fine plush seats that, for a modest extra fee, could be converted into snug berths at night. They reveled in such amenities as steam heating, fresh linen daily and fancy furnishings. And they were served by porters and fatherly conductors who catered to their wishes and whims. For an extra charge of about $4 a day, a first-class passenger in 1870 could take the weekly Pacific Hotel Express that offered dining on board. Unless they rode this special train, first- and second-class passengers alike took their meals on the run at stops along the way. On the Hotel Express trains, the level of food and service was equal to that of the best restaurants of the day, and the trip from the Missouri to the Pacific could be a constant lark or a restful four-day vacation.

Second-class passengers, riding in day coaches, had a different time of it. They moved with the speed of the express, but enjoyed only a small measure of the comfort and no splendor at all. Their coaches were upholstered, but they slept in their seats, if they slept at all. For the complete Omaha-to-Sacramento trip they paid $80—and did not seem to feel cheated.

The reason was simple: most of them were not making the complete run, and therefore not paying the fare for it. Day coaches were the place for "way" or short-haul passengers—the cowhands, farmers, miners, hunters and Indians who made up the permanent population of the West. Typically, they rode a few miles or hundreds of miles down the line. According to one account, no less than 230 stations, most of them in tank towns and whistle stops, dotted the long Western route; and from the beginning, trips between them exceeded through-passenger traffic. In 1870 there were one fourth more way passengers than through passengers

For Easterners who had never seen a buffalo in their lives, an avidly wished-for experience on a transcontinental trip came when a whole herd of the animals blocked a train, as depicted here by artist Newbold Trotter. Many passengers brought guns and took potshots at the hulking creatures.

137

The Northern Pacific boasted its route traversed a land as wondrous as that of Lewis Carroll's Alice—and in an 1885 tourist brochure a copywriter had "Alice" describe the enticements of an N.P. rail journey.

NORTHERN PACIFIC R.R. THE WONDERLAND Route to the PACIFIC COAST

CHAS.S.FEE Gen'l.Pass.Agent ST. PAUL.

Alice's Adventures IN THE NEW WONDERLAND The Yellowstone National Park

POOLE BROS PRINTERS AND ENGRAVERS, CHICAGO.

MAMMOTH HOT SPRINGS HOTEL, NATIONAL PARK, WYOMING TERRITORY, U. S., Sept. 2d, 1885.

MY DEAREST EDITH:

When Mr. Carroll wrote that funny book about one of my childish dreams, I little thought the time would ever come when I should sit down to describe scenes and incidents in my actual experience every bit as strange and bewildering. Yet, so it is. I am here in a place which, singularly enough, they call Wonderland. Not that that title is by any means inappropriate, for the place is, indeed, a land of wonders; but the coincidence, at least, is somewhat remarkable, for you know what the associations of that word "Wonderland" are to me. Well, here I am, rubbing my eyes every day, to be sure that I am not either in a dream or in a new world. You never saw, nor could you ever imagine, such strange sights as greet us here at every turn. It is not only that everything is big; that is characteristic of the whole country, everything in nature being on a much larger scale than we are accustomed to in Europe. But besides the Rocky mountains and a waterfall—and a big one too, twice as high as Niagara—there is the grandest old lot of geysers and boiling springs in the world, and a river shut in for several miles of its course by mountains rising hundreds of feet above it, what they call a cañon (pronounced canyon), the walls of which are of such glowing colors that papa said he could compare it to nothing but the most gorgeous sunset he had ever seen. Then, what with the action of fire and water, the appearance of the earth itself is very curious; but I suppose that, as it will be two months at least before we get home, I had better give you a more detailed account of our journey since I wrote you from Chicago. We left that city in the evening for St. Paul, where we arrived the following afternoon. We found St. Paul such a beautiful city. It is built for the most part on the side of a hill overlooking the Mississippi river. It is the capital of the State of Minnesota and contains many fine buildings. Within twenty minutes' ride by train there is another large city named Minneapolis, where there are the biggest corn mills, as we should call them, in the world. They call them flouring mills, for, as you probably know, the word corn is not applied in this country to different kinds of grain, as it is in England, but only to what we call maize or Indian corn. When they

from Omaha to California; by the early 1880s short-haul travelers outnumbered the long-hauls six to one.

The day-coach riders invariably fascinated visitors from Eastern states and foreign countries. Often they were the first—and sometimes the last—real Westerners these visitors ever saw, and they carried with them an air of the exotic frontier that enthralled all the rest of the world. Henryk Sienkiewicz, a Polish novelist who toured the West in 1876, described them with awe and a touch of fear: "They are not elegant, carefully dressed gentlemen, but bearded and mustached individuals dressed in ragged garments, carrying dirty bundles, and with revolvers stuck in their belts. Their talk is loud and stormy and filled with profanity. Clouds of tobacco smoke rise to the ceiling of the coaches. Doors slam as they are opened and closed by strong hands.

References to the Sioux and Pawnees, Indian tribes inhabiting Nebraska and the Dakotas, are frequently heard in the conversation."

While the day-coach passengers generally represented the real West, the third and lowest class of passengers stood for a West that was still aborning. Typically, they were emigrants, outward bound to settle the vast empty lands owned by the railroads and the federal government. From Eastern and Midwestern states—and then, increasingly from the countries of western and northern Europe—the emigrants came in search of land, or wealth, or simply a life more bearable than the one they had left behind. But their first glimpse of their new lives was frequently discouraging.

Emigrants paid about $40 for a transcontinental trip—the lowest fare for the worst accommodations. Their

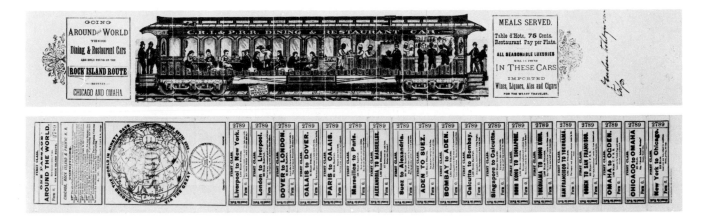

cars, fitted with rows of narrow wooden benches, were often coupled to freight cars, and they were constantly shunted aside to make way for the expresses. Thus the westward trip from Omaha, which took four to four and a half days for the swells, might last nine, 10 or more days for the emigrants. And every one of those days had hours of boredom and discomfort. The emigrants endured the journey because they had to.

First-class passengers, by contrast, took their trips largely for pleasure. Almost as soon as the rails were joined at Promontory, no man of the world considered himself well traveled until he went across America in the steam cars. Given such clientele, the Western lines cosseted the well-heeled, high-paying passengers. And the cosseting was made extravagant by the ministrations of George Mortimer Pullman, a builder of railroad cars who had long recognized the profit potential in providing creature comforts for those who could afford it.

As early as 1864, in Chicago, Pullman had developed the two most significant and lasting contributions to comfortable day-and-night accommodations: a hinged upper berth, well upholstered, that could be folded against the ceiling of the car, and hinged seats and seat backs that could be flattened for night travel. By the time transcontinental railroading became a reality, he was making himself the unchallengeable feudal lord of restful travel, and the long Western train trips provided an ideal opportunity for his special brand of luxury. From the start, he was able to lease to the Western lines cars that were fully equipped and staffed.

But the sleeping car represented only part of George Pullman's contribution. His parlor cars were resplendent in plush upholstery, rich hangings and hand-carved inlaid paneling. And his magnificent dining cars, in which first-class passengers ate meals prepared by Pullman chefs and served by Pullman waiters, offered a measure of high living unprecedented until then.

Pullman named his first dining car the *Delmonico,* after a famous gourmet restaurant in New York City, and he set appropriately high standards in his food. For a holiday feast in the West, a Pullman staff was capable of turning out a 12-course dinner equal to that of the finest big-city restaurants of the day *(pages 164-165).* Everyday meals were less sumptuous, of course; but almost all the first-class passengers, including the ladies, boasted of gaining five to 10 pounds aboard a Hotel Express on a special one-month round trip between Cincinnati and San Francisco. And well they might. The dishes regularly provided passengers on these special trains included blue-winged teal, antelope steaks, roast beef, boiled ham and tongue, broiled chicken, corn on the cob, fresh fruit, hot rolls, corn bread and, everywhere in the Rockies, fresh trout.

But until the late 1880s, when dining cars became available on regular express trains, most passengers who traveled by rail out West took their meals at stations along the way. Meals were adequate but lacked variety. Susan Coolidge, in a magazine article describing travel west in 1873, claimed that "it was necessary to look at one's watch to tell whether it was breakfast, dinner or supper, these meals presenting invariably the same salient features of beefsteak, fried eggs, fried potato." Two relatively mild and quite untypical complaints about food were recorded by early passengers. One, having had a "delicious chicken stew" for breakfast, was later disturbed to learn he had eaten prairie dog. Another pas-

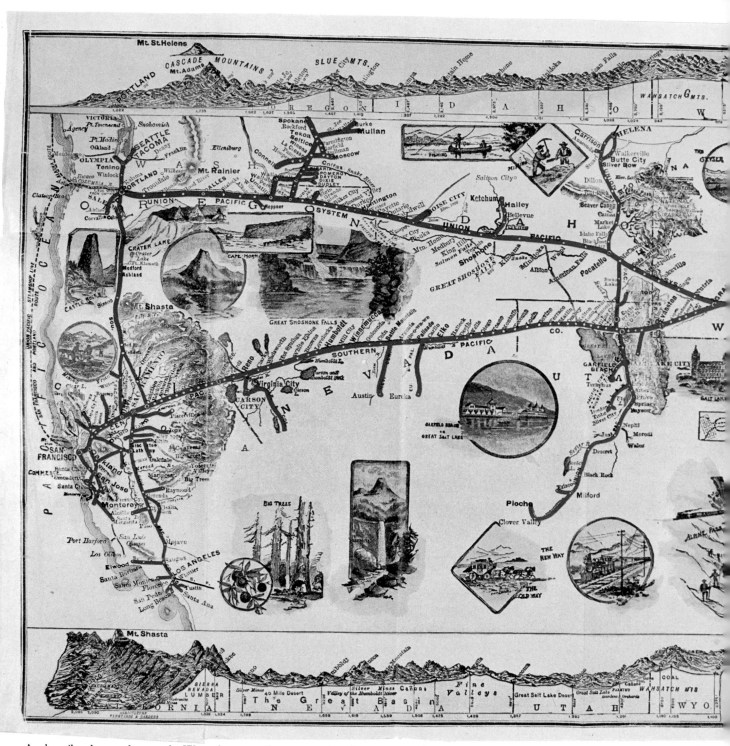

As the railroads spread across the West, they opened up an ever broader panorama of scenic marvels. By 1893, the Union Pacific was using this

senger, after a dreary day of riding through the desert-like Great Basin, was offered a meal of freshly shot plover. Upon being told that plover was a game bird, he refused the dish on the grounds that a winged animal too stupid to fly away from such a desolate place was "unfit for human food."

The first-class passenger had plenty of alternatives to his own comfortable seat. For one thing, he had complete freedom of the train, and he usually reveled in it.

A second-class passenger might not have been permitted to observe life inside a Pullman even from the respectful distance of a doorway. But no such prohibition was imposed on Pullman passengers, and they often were drawn by a combination of curiosity and condescension to inspect their humbler fellow travelers.

In 1877 a luxurious railroad junket to the West was led by the millionaire newspaper publisher Frank Leslie, traveling in his own private hotel car. He was ac-

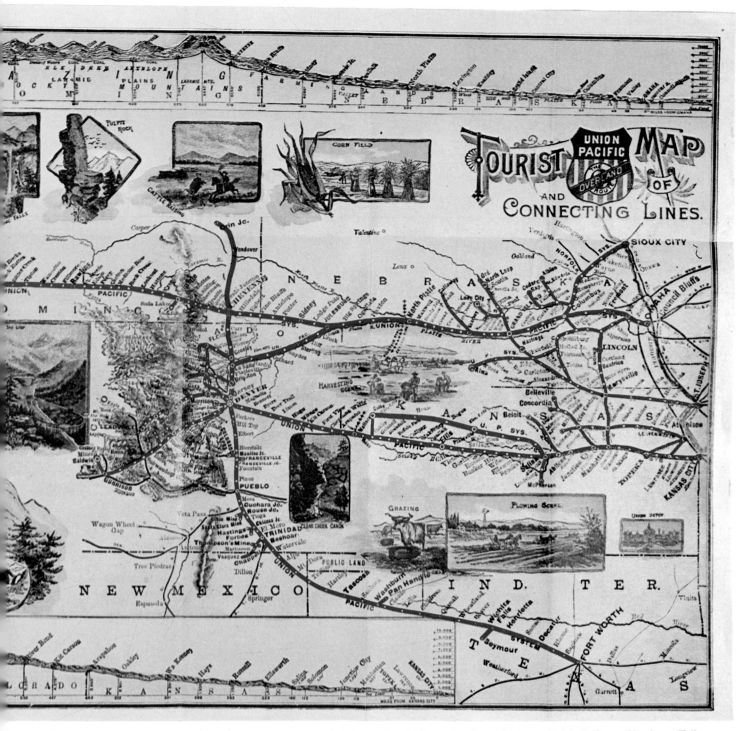

pictorial map to advertise such attractions along its route as the Salt Lake City Tabernacle, Crater Lake and Idaho's Great Shoshone Falls.

companied by sketch artists, photographers and a pair of star reporters, as befitted the host's profession *(page 128)*. During the trip, one reporter described another car on the same train—a first-class car, but one well below the sumptuous standards of the Leslie travelers.

"A consumptive invalid bent double in a paroxysm of coughing; four parties, invisible but palpable to the touch, are wrestling in the agonies of the toilet behind closely buttoned curtains and trampling on the toes of passers-by. Two young lovers are exchanging endearments in a remote corner. Who could bear these things with perfect equanimity? Who could rise under the close personal scrutiny of twenty-nine fellow beings without being ready to charge one's soul with twenty-nine distinct homicides?"

Turning to still less fortunate travelers, the reporter wrote: "And what about the ordinary passenger car, wherein the working-men and working-women—the

141

miners, gold seekers, trappers, hunters and queer back-woods folk—congregate, all packed like sardines in a box? It is pathetic to see the vain attempts to improvise out of their two or three feet of space a comfortable sleeping place for some sick girl or feeble old person. Every seat has its occupant, by night as well as day, a congregation of aching spines."

The Leslie expedition was not the earliest elite excursion to the coast. Amid much fanfare the first such trip was put together in 1870 by the Boston Board of Trade, with an eye not only to fashionable adventure but also to exploring the possibilities of profitable commerce with the West Coast. The group included 129 social, political and commercial luminaries led by Alexander Rice, later a governor of Massachusetts. They took along a "brand-new quarto-medium Gordon printing press" and an eloquent editor named W. R. Steele, and published a daily newspaper en route.

The party traveled in a special train of eight cars, all built by George M. Pullman: two so-called hotel cars, the *Revere* and the *Arlington,* appointed for both dining and sleeping; two sleeping and drawing-room cars, the *Palmyra* and the *Marquette;* two commissary cars named *St. Cloud* and *St. Charles;* a baggage car fitted with five iceboxes; and a four-room smoking car that also included the editorial and printing office, whose type cases were made of fine black walnut. As befitted a Boston group, the train carried two excellent classical libraries. Fifty thousand Bostonians toured the train before it left and hundreds cheered it off.

The trip itself had its own excitements—and its disappointments. The travelers longed for a glimpse of the enormous herds of buffalo that, they had long believed, blackened the Western prairies. They did see a few herds here and there but the buffalo was no longer present in myriads; thousands of them had been slaughtered to feed the hungry crews who built the very railroad on which the Bostonians were traveling. (Other lines were equally profligate; over a period of eight months, Buffalo Bill Cody singlehandedly killed some 4,300 buffalo for the Kansas Pacific Railroad, at a net cost to the company of one cent per pound of meat.)

On the other hand, the New Englanders loved their train and its fittings, and they dearly loved the experience of traveling on that train. The children in the party played leapfrog in one of the saloon cars—ac-

On early Western railroads, a stop for refreshments often lasted 10 minutes. In the helter-skelter, as this A & P advertisement shows, a second cupful of coffee was hard to come by, even for a passenger who beseeched a waiter's attention from a soapbox. Usually travelers had to pay when they ordered; some caterers bribed conductors to cut the stop short so that uneaten —but paid for—snacks could be saved.

Fred Harvey's gallant girls and fine food

Frederick Henry Harvey rescued late 19th Century railway travelers from the horrors of depot meals *(see preceding page)* through a novel combination of good food and good girls.

When Harvey left London to seek his fortune in the New World the year was 1850 and he was just 15. Twenty-six years later, after a wandering career that included running his own restaurant and working on several railroads, Harvey assumed the management of the Topeka depot restaurant on the Santa Fe line. There he proved to be the right man in the right place at the right time. Harvey soon became the concessionaire for all the meals served along the Santa Fe system, employing railroad premises and equipment, and supplying both the food and service. Eventually he commanded a catering empire of 47 depot diners and restaurants, 15 railroad hotels and 30 dining cars. And for the first time in the West, a railroad became famous for its food.

Harvey operated with a high hand. If he found a chipped cup he might dash a whole table setting to the floor. When skylarking cowboys rode their ponies right into a Harvey House, Harvey dismissed them with a few cool words. They were readmitted only after dismounting and donning neat alpaca jackets, which the host kept on hand for the coatless. (As one cowboy said to his bunkhouse comrades: "They make you take off your hat and put on a coat, but the grub is strictly A-No. 1.")

To his fine food Harvey quickly added a daring new attraction—waitresses. His advertisements for "young

Comely Harvey Girls, simply but attractively dressed, take a break at Rosenberg, Texas.

women of good character, attractive and intelligent, 18 to 30" brought in droves of them at a salary of $17.50 a month plus board, room and tips. Living in a Harvey dormitory with a chaperoned courting parlor and a 10 o'clock curfew, a thrifty girl could soon save up a tidy dowry for herself.

The crisply aproned Harvey Girls dazzled lonely Westerners, who married an estimated 5,000 of them. "A fairer maiden I shall never see," wrote a contemporary poet of a Harvey Girl. "She was winsome, she was neat, she was gloriously sweet and she certainly was very good to me."

companied, according to editor Steele's dry comment, by "some of a larger growth." The grownups, Steele noted, made themselves at home in their "moving hotel." "They read, write and talk in their parlors; they sing and play in the saloons, and they move from car to car with freedom."

At one point on the plains, some of the ladies and children adopted a docile young antelope, and took the bewildered animal along as a pet over 2,000 miles of track—until it sickened and was put off the train. In the *Palmyra,* an audience "limited only by the capacity of the car" gathered for evening services, complete with hymn singing, an organ accompaniment and a sermon on "the wonders and mercies shown us during our eventful journey." In sharp contrast to this spiritual exercise, the Bostonians solemnly tested the technology surrounding them. Telegraph wires had been strung along the right of way as the tracks advanced, and telegraph operators were available at many stations along the route. One member of the party dispatched a telegram home inquiring after the health of his wife, and editor Steele testified in his newspaper that "we had run scarce 47 miles" before an answer came in.

The Boston group was followed in a few weeks by a delegation of 53 solid citizens representing the Chamber of Commerce of Cincinnati. Their Hotel Express included a car that "in the daytime is an elegant saloon, fitted up with sofas on either side, leaving ample space for dancing. Built into the car is a fine parlor organ which, under the fingers of some passenger, furnishes the music for a cotillion." By and large, the expedition patriotically reported, their cars "would make the eyes of an Englishman pop painfully on beholding the triumphs of American railroading genius. The sleeping cars are fitted up with oiled walnut, carved and gilded, etched and stained plate glass, metal trappings heavily silver-plated, seats cushioned with thick plushes, washstands of marble and walnut, damask curtains, and massive mirrors in frames of gilded walnut. The floors are carpeted with the most costly Brussels, and the roof beautifully frescoed in mosaics of gold, emerald-green, crimson, sky-blue, violet, drab and black."

In this magnificent setting, the Cincinnatians amused themselves by planning and carrying out amateur theatricals. Other excursionists, they noted, had enjoyed "banquets, concerts and social entertainments on cars

running twenty-five or thirty miles an hour, but the Cincinnati company took a long stride ahead by giving two highly successful exhibitions of *tableaux vivants.*" As the party sped over the Rocky Mountains, "six to seven thousand feet above the sea and fifteen hundred miles west of Cincinnati," one of the cars was darkened. An improvised curtain of striped damask parted to reveal a mattress-covered stage about six feet deep.

Before a rapt audience, some members of the party took poses as living statues in eight witty scenes. The subjects included "Woman's Rights" and "Domestic Infelicity, Caused by Too Much Chess-Playing," followed by a "Grand Musical Finale." Not only was a good time had by all, but all agreed that this railroad performance constituted "the first of the kind ever witnessed on this planet."

At one point the Cincinnatians were exposed to a railroading tragedy. The fireman, a young man named James Wilson Collins, "fell under the wheels while attempting to detach the caboose from the tender. The caboose passed over his right arm and both legs above the knees. Dr. W. T. Brown, one of the excursionists, labored for several hours to alleviate the poor man's sufferings. His injuries were fatal and he soon passed into the coma that precedes death. He knew eternity was at hand but feared nothing."

In their preoccupation with such excitements of the journey, the Cincinnati ladies did not neglect the daily necessities of dealing with cinders, smoke, baking sun, rain and the dust of the Western prairies. One thoughtfully advised the official chronicler of the trip to warn other women contemplating the Western adventure to bring "an entire change of linen in a hand valise to be carried in the sleeping coach. Dresses should be of gray or brown worsted—never black. A linen duster of ample size is essential." The mention of linen dusters and the solemn warning that they formed an essential part of a lady's wardrobe recur constantly in such accounts. Susan Coolidge, in her magazine article, spelled out the main reason for taking them along: "Dust is the great foe to comfort on the Pacific Railroad. No brushing, no shaking removes it. It sifts, it penetrates, it pervades everywhere. After two or three days you grow to hate yourself."

The Cincinnati lady also took compassionate thought to warn others of illnesses they might expect on trips

Typical of Western railroad stations, the Santa Fe depot at Topeka became the busiest place in town when a train was due—partly because the train's arrival was the day's biggest excitement. Trains paused while passengers ate in the first Harvey House Dining Hall at the end of the station.

147

Usually inelegant in design but always close to the train station, hotels gave rudimentary lodging to passengers waiting overnight to change trains.

This establishment, photographed about 1880, was in Colorado's Central City and depended for business on the Colorado Central Railroad.

readily forget. I passed to and fro, stepping across the prostrate, and caught now a snore, now a gasp, now a half-formed word, it gave me a measure of the worthlessness of rest in that unresting vehicle. Although it was chill, I was obliged to open my window, for the degradation of the air soon became intolerable. Outside I saw the black amorphous hills shoot by unweariedly into our wake. They that long for morning have never longed for it more earnestly than I."

On another occasion he retired to the end of his car and tried to take his mind off his wretchedness by reading a book. To get some fresh air, he held the car door open with a foot protruding into the aisle. The news butcher, of course, was busy plying his trade. Whenever he passed Stevenson's refuge, he kicked the exposed foot. "I tell about this," Stevenson confided to his journal, "because it gives so good an example of that uncivil kindness of the American, which is perhaps their most bewildering character. On these occasions he most rudely struck my foot aside; and though I myself apologized, he answered me never a word. I chafed furiously, but suddenly I felt a touch upon my shoulder, and a large juicy pear was put into my hand. It was the newsboy, who had observed that I was looking ill, and so made me this present out of a tender heart."

No man in Stevenson's condition could reasonably be expected to take note of the passing scene or to be much engaged by anything other than his own miseries and the common discomfort of his emigrant car. Most of what he saw outside seemed to him simply dreary, particularly during the long crossing of the slowly rising country leading toward the Rocky Mountains.

"At sea on the plains of Nebraska," he noted, "I made my observatory on the top of a fruit-waggon, and sat by the hour upon that perch to spy about me, and to spy in vain for something new. It was a world almost without feature; an empty sky, an empty earth; front and back, the line of railway stretched from horizon to horizon. On either hand, the green plain ran till it touched the skirts of heaven. The train toiled over this infinity like a snail." At the sight of a scattering of houses in a tiny town, he mused, "the mind is loath to accept it for a piece of reality; and it seems incredible that life can go on with so few properties, or that the great child, man, finds entertainment in so bare a playroom."

But while Stevenson gazed about him in boredom and reckoned himself "more dead than alive," other wayfarers on the Western rails found their journeys a source of endless fascination and some occasional terror. Few traveled those iron roads unmoved by one circumstance or another. William Lawrence Humason, who was one of the first of these travelers (his transcontinental train arrived at Promontory less than a week after the driving of the golden spike), suffered just about everything that a new railroad built in competitive frenzy could offer and he, too, recorded his experience.

As the train toiled up the high Wyoming slope, Humason encountered that rarity, a drunken engineer—or so he suspected, although Humason admitted that he could not prove it. Certainly the hand on the throttle gave him a restless night, with sudden stops, race-horse starts and wild dashes "as though demons were in pursuit of him," until the train had to make long stops to let the flaming boxes cool off.

Next day Humason's train stopped at a country station. The platform was crowded with men brandishing pistols, rifles and shotguns. Humason was told that these men were vigilantes who had, the day before, strung up a local citizen upon a telegraph pole for "committing a fiendish outrage upon the only respectable woman in the place." Now, he was told, the rapist's friends were coming to board the train and "wipe out the place" to avenge him, and the vigilantes were there to see that they did not succeed.

This excitement was soon followed by a new one when the train began rolling downslope. Part of the roadbed had been hastily built on frozen ground the winter before by Union Pacific track crews. Spring floods and melting frost had undermined it and "the cars were rocking and bounding in a very unsatisfactory manner.

We thought there was danger to be apprehended from so great a speed on such a rough road, but the conductor said he had never run off the track yet."

Shortly afterward the train did exactly that. Humason and some fellow passengers dashed for brakes and bell cord to warn the engineer. The derailed cars went bumping and bucking over the ties, "breaking many of them as though they were but pipe-stems," then finally stopped just short of the edge of an embankment. "Now came the excitement, the screaming, the shouting and the weeping—not unmingled with some earnest prayers. All who remained on the car were uninjured; but one passenger had leaped from the rear of the car and struck upon his head, creating an ugly-looking wound, from which he has not yet fully recovered."

Next day the train arrived at Weber Canyon in the Wasatch mountains. Humason had time to study what he called the "wonderful cannon," for his train "ran very slow, to avoid another accident." With a curious mixture of delight and fear, he described the "high mountains faced with perpendicular rocks, carved in fantastic shapes of castles, profiles, pulpits, stairs, slides, etc. Little streams, fed by the melting snows which accumulate in the recesses of the mountains, fall over the lofty heights into the Weber below. As you look up from the side of the deep cannon thousands of feet, great masses of rocks appear as though the least jar or sound would send them crashing down upon your head."

No rock crashed down, but Humason's fears proved well founded. The train soon came to a wooden bridge, stretching high in the air from cliff to cliff, so weakened by the spring flood in the Weber River that not even that daredevil engineer would risk a train full of passengers upon it. Eventually their locomotive, "old 121," was pushed across the creaking trestle at the head of a string of expendable flatcars. When that experiment succeeded, the empty passenger cars were brought across with greater confidence. But some of the passengers made a scary passage afoot, "stepping from tie to tie. A single misstep would have sent us down where no human arm could rescue; and where one poor fellow, the next day, went and returned not." With the peril survived, Humason and his companions got back aboard and were on their way again.

Two hazards to which most westward travelers looked forward in shuddery anticipation were Indians

155

Snowslides and snowdrifts as deep as 30 feet, and temperatures that reached 35° below zero, imperiled passengers on Western railroads during half the year. This slide in the Cascade foothills buried three engines.

and highwaymen. Happily, most travelers were disappointed, particularly by the Indians, who were rapidly running out of the will to tackle what Robert Louis Stevenson called the white man's "bad medicine-wagon."

Humason, one of the earliest to report the scene, came frighteningly close to running afoul of live and angry warriors. A band of them, he said, had raided one railway station and made off with some livestock on the night before his arrival there. From his train he did manage to see some Indians who, he supposed, were "about to take the warpath, hideous in paint and feathers." He prophetically noted that "our cavalry cannot operate successfully against these Indians in the summer, when their horses are in good condition. They must be hunted in winter. The poor Indian has few friends and his days will soon be numbered."

To another early traveler on the Western rails, the Reverend Samuel Bowles, who also went across the country late in 1869, the sight of a half dozen U.S. Army troopers lining up at several Wyoming stations suggested that "the Indian question is not disposed of yet," but Bowles saw no hostiles in the flesh. The Polish novelist Henryk Sienkiewicz also failed to witness any actual violence at the hands of Indians, but at a station in a small town in Iowa he believed he saw convincing evidence of past crimes among a half dozen aging Sioux warriors. At their belts, he wrote, "hung scalps, that is, hair together with the skin torn from the heads of their enemies; human hair also decorated the seams of their garments."

The Frank Leslie party also got a firsthand look at an exhibit indicating that the Indians were not always as peaceful as those seen at railroad stations seemed to be. Leslie's train had just taken on a new train crew in the Black Hills when one of the Pullman passengers cried, "Here's a scalped man—a conductor—but don't look at him because he doesn't like it!" Naturally, everybody aboard promptly stared at the man, a conductor named Tommy Cahoon. Years earlier, Sioux warriors had lifted Cahoon's hair while he was innocently fishing in a creek near Cheyenne, Wyoming, but they had unaccountably neglected to kill him. Persuaded by the passengers, Cahoon doffed his conductor's cap and showed his scarred and naked scalp.

"Wouldn't you like to have *your* way with those fellows just once?" one of the dudes asked. And with the

More frightening to rail passengers than the deepest snow, more threatening than bandits was the prairie fire, which could engulf hundreds of square miles. Fires might blaze up from smokestack sparks, but some were lit by Indians bent on driving the white man and his works off the land.

To lure the carriage trade into taking the long trip West, railroads offered genteel comforts such as this reclining chair, designed in 1876 and adopted by George Pullman for his luxurious first-class cars.

wisdom of experience, Cahoon replied: "Well *my* way would be to give 'em a pretty wide berth."

Women usually expressed interest in the Indian manner of carrying their young bundled in papoose baskets strapped to their back. One voyager, Helen Hunt Jackson—who was later to write *Ramona*, a moving novel of Indian life—made a sharp distinction between an Indian mother and her child. The mother, she wrote, seemed to her "the most abject, loathly living thing I ever saw." But she saw on her back, "gleaming out from under a ragged calash-like arch of basketwork, a smooth, shining, soft baby face, brown as a brown nut, silken as silk, sweet, happy, innocent, confiding, as if it were babe of a royal line, borne in royal state."

On the whole, robbers did better than Indians in providing adventure-minded travelers with memorable experiences. In 1882 a British passenger named T. S. Hudson got close enough to a train holdup to give him something to think about. Down in the Southwest near Tucson, on the Southern Pacific line, Hudson noticed that "the cars were very sparsely peopled, recent robberies of trains by desperadoes, and the unsettled state of the Indian population, having made the route temporarily unpopular. A short time previously the engineer and fireman had been killed by a gang of robbers, and the treasure in the express van had only been saved by the heroic conduct of the passengers in driving off the marauders. A male *compagnon de voyage* asked me in some trepidation whether I was aware that there were only twenty-five persons of our gender in the train. I could only reply that in the records of recent car robberies it appeared that the ladies, of whom we had a goodly number as bodyguard, had always figured as the braver part of the company."

Clearly, the possibility of falling into the hands of train robbers was real enough in those times. One Central Pacific train had the singular bad luck to be held up twice in two days at ambushes 400 miles apart. The first robbery took place after six strangers boarded an eastbound train at Truckee, California, at one o'clock in the morning. When the train pulled in at Verdi, 22 miles down the track on the California-Nevada border, two of the men went forward along the cars and got the drop on the engineer and fireman. The other four broke into the express car and made off with cash and bullion valued at $40,000, an extraordinarily good haul. The second holdup, which the C.P.'s men reckoned as an abuse of the privilege of being outrageous, took place near Toana, Nevada. Neither set of bandits was apprehended. Those who knew their way around those parts believed that the second holdup was the work of a local gambler named Jack Davis, who was considered a leading citizen because of his generosity to the poor but is otherwise unknown to history.

One Western train robber who did win his way into the immortality of legend and balladry was a colorful character from Indiana by the name of Sam Bass. A man of expensive tastes in race horses, booze and fancy women, Sam began his career by robbing stage coaches in the Black Hills. Scenting bigger game in the iron horse, he and a gang of five men in 1877 knocked off the express car of a Union Pacific train at Big Springs, Nebraska. The job paid handsomely—$60,000. Encouraged, Sam went on to hold up one Houston & Texas Central and Texas & Pacific train after another. But he never struck it rich again; one robbery yielded him $52. Finally, at Round Rock, Texas, a Texas Ranger killed him. He was 27 years old at the time.

Two facts about Bass appealed to the popular imagination. First, he was a generous fellow, paying as much as half a dollar for a chew of tobacco and a $20 gold piece for a panful of hot biscuits when he was on the run from the law. Second, he was said to have a habit of burying his loot in unlikely places. Armed with maps or bits of folklore, people searching for the loot were still digging up odd cellars and chopping down hollow trees 50 years after his death. Nobody ever found Sam's trove, if indeed it ever existed. But his fame was such

Victorian elegance marked private Pullmans, which bore names, like ships. The Countess, shown here, offered de luxe living at $50 a day.

A drawing from an 1879 manual for railroad-car builders depicts George Pullman's ingenious design for sleeping in transit. An upper berth, shown open, is suspended by chains from the car's ceiling. The lower berth will be set up by removing the table and rearranging the two facing seats.

that some unknown minstrels composed a folk ballad about him. One climactic stanza about Sam and one of his gang, Frank Jackson, runs like this:

Sam met his fate at Round Rock, July the twenty-first.
They dropped the boy with rifle balls
and then they took his purse,
Poor Sam he is a dead lad, and six foot under clay,
And Jackson's in the mesquite aiming to get away.

Transcontinental tourists were glad to escape the attentions of the likes of Sam Bass—but there was little else they wanted to be spared. Most of them, and particularly the passengers who rode first class, came out to see everything they could see. One sight they wanted a good look at was the polygamous Mormons in and around Salt Lake City. Therefore, most posh tourists left the railroad at Ogden for Brigham Young's capital. Until a connecting line was built in 1870, they rode a stagecoach some 40 miles over a potholed road.

One of the first travelers to observe the Mormons on their home turf was W. L. Humason. Already much tried by his adventures on the new iron track, Humason relaxed and found new fascination here. He was permitted to attend services in the enormous domed Mormon Tabernacle and learned that strictures laid upon the Latter-day Saints by their elders were, in some respects, more demanding than those of puritan New England. The men, he said, were taught to renounce such gentile foibles as "tight, fine-textured pants with broad stripes, and silk stovepipe hats; while the women were exhorted to nurse their own babies." Like many visitors, Humason was determined to penetrate the Mormon practice of polygamy. He came to the conclusion that polygamy fostered an iniquitous monopoly by which the more prosperous Mormons "take advantage of the situation, selecting all the young and pretty women, leaving the poor young man who sighs like a furnace to take the old and ugly."

Other tourists restricted their condescending observations to the outward appearance of the Mormons. A reporter with Frank Leslie's party, for example, had this to report: "Our first impressions of Mormondon are not seductive. There is a family likeness in them all; the lean, tough, hard-worked man, with uncouthly cut hair, and skin like tanned leather; the woman on each arm, in her old-time calico gown and shawl, with her sunburnt, subdued and hopelessly and invariably plain face crowned by a marvel of a hat—an erection of yellow straw, red and blue roses and marvelous phenomena in the shape of feathers."

One and all, of course, were avid to know how many wives had been accumulated by the leader of the flock, Brigham Young. But Young, one suspects, had grown a little weary of the question. He told a prying Cincinnati lady he had absentmindedly mislaid the family register. To others, he gave a precise figure of 16 wives and 49 children. But it did not really matter what he said. Consciously or not, most gentile visitors were scurrilous in their comments. Almost without exception, they approached Salt Lake City with a sense of anticipatory horror at the thought of goatish Mormons accompanied by numerous and willing women.

The novelist Helen Hunt Jackson took a somewhat different view of the matter. She observed that Salt Lake City was clean, orderly, beautifully planned and planted, and prosperous. Inquiring more deeply, she came upon "the strongest testimony to the uprightness,

honesty, industry, purity of Mormon lives, and their charity also." In spite of the presence of polygamy, which she found oppressive, she wrote: "You look earnestly into the faces of all the women you see. They are standing on doorsills, with laughing babies in their arms; they are talking gayly with each other. They are walking by the side of men; they are carrying burdens, or seeking pleasure, just as other women do—apparently." And having delivered herself of these observations, she made her way back to Ogden.

At Ogden—or, earlier, at Promontory—westbound passengers switched from the Union Pacific to the Central Pacific line, and first-class passengers moved from Pullman Palace into Silver Palace cars. Though Ogden was a thriving Mormon town, Promontory never did amount to much more than a meeting place of rails. At its best, it consisted of a railroad station and express office on one side of a track and a huddle of one-story, canvas-roofed structures on the other, all occupied by various businesses. Among its amenities were a couple

of three-card-monte and crap games for the fleecing of visitors (three members of the party from Cincinnati managed to lose about $120 in 30 minutes there). Yet, for the traveler, the transfer at Promontory or Ogden brought more of a change than might be expected, and for Robert Louis Stevenson the change came none too soon. The cars "in which we had been cooped for more than ninety hours had begun to stink abominably. I have stood on a platform while the whole train was shunting, and, as the dwelling-cars drew near, there would come a whiff of pure menagerie, only a little sourer, as from men instead of monkeys. I think we are human only in virtue of open windows."

He was about to get some relief. The Central Pacific's emigrant cars were nearly twice as tall as those of the U.P., with a capacity for twice as much air. Stevenson was able to discard his bed board, since seats in these cars could be pulled out and joined in the center to make room for lying down at night. Moreover, the C.P. provided a crude version of upper berths, con-

163

The ultimate in sumptuous railroad eating was this Christmas dinner aboard the Chicago and North Western. A menu with an elaborate cover *(below)* offered 12 courses and 45 dishes *(right)* to choose from.

sisting of wooden shelves that could be closed out of the way in the daytime. This last luxury, however, turned out to be a cruel snare, "for it fell to me to sleep in one of the lofts; and that I found to be impossible. The air was always bad enough at the level of the floor. But my bed was four feet higher, immediately under the roof, and shut into a kind of Saratoga trunk. It were at that level madness to attempt to sleep."

For one first-class passenger, the switch from the Union Pacific's Pullman Palace cars to the Central Pacific's Silver Palace sleepers turned out to be dismal in every way. Helen Hunt Jackson, in her straightforward way, admitted: "It is impossible to be just to a person or a thing disliked. I dislike the sleeping car sections more than I ever have disliked, ever shall dislike, or ever can dislike anything in the world."

She was 48 years old at the time, which entitles her to some sympathy for the gymnastic contortions im-

posed on her by her berth. The problem turned upon a clash between modesty and muscle —a clash in which both came out losers. Complicating factors were curtains too short to reach both the middle and the ends, panels of wood overhead so beautifully polished that they served as a mirror to reveal everything in the next bunk, and the fact that the occupant of the next berth was an otherwise obliging "English gentleman."

Mrs. Jackson made her first mistake by getting half undressed after she had stowed some of her things under her berth. They could not be reached without getting out into the aisle, lying prone and reaching under the berth. To make matters worse, the only way to sit in the berth without dangling one's legs in the aisle was cross-legged and the posture was agonizing. She also found that the curtains around the berth simply didn't fit, even when anchored to the mattress and pillow with pins. No sooner was she settled for the night than the

Christmas Dinner—1890.

— • —

BLUE POINTS.

GREEN TURTLE.   OX TAIL.

BOILED CALIFORNIA SALMON, WITH FRENCH PEAS.
BAKED RED SNAPPER—PIQUANTE SAUCE.

MUTTON—CAPER SAUCE.   CAPON—EGG SAUCE.

BEEF.
TURKEY—STUFFED WITH CHESTNUTS.

GOOSE—APPLE SAUCE.   DUCK—CURRANT JELLY.
ROAST QUAIL—STUFFED.   WILD TURKEY—GRAPE JELLY.
GROUSE MACEDONIA STYLE.

SWEETBREADS -POTTED -SMOTHERED WITH MUSHROOMS.
BAKED RABBIT PIE—AMERICAN STYLE.
CROQUETTES OF OYSTERS.
ORANGE FRITTERS.   CHICORY AND LOBSTER SALAD.

CELERY.   LETTUCE.   CHOW CHOW.   QUEEN OLIVES.

MASHED POTATOES.   BOILED SWEET POTATOES.
ASPARAGUS.   STEWED TOMATOES.
GREEN PEAS.   GREEN CORN.

ENGLISH PLUM PUDDING—BRANDY SAUCE.   COCOANUT PUDDING—WINE SAUCE.
MINCE AND PUMPKIN PIE.
CHARLOTTE RUSSE.

NEW YORK ICE CREAM.   LEMON ICE.   CAKE
EDAM AND ROQUEFORT CHEESE.   BENT'S CRACKERS.
COFFEE.

MALAGA AND CATAWBA GRAPES.
ORANGES.   BANANAS   APPLES.
ASSORTED NUTS.   RAISINS.

train lurched and threw her out of the berth and into the arms of the English gentleman, who was threading his way along the aisle. "Being an English gentleman, he would look the other way if he could, but how can he? He must hold you up! Nothing seems very clear to you for some minutes except the English gentleman's face, which is indelibly stamped on your brain."

She fell asleep at last — or at least lapsed into a coma brought on by frustration and despair. But she awoke to what she described as a "new perplexity." Just above her was the English gentleman's florid face, adorned by a red silk kerchief about his brow. As Mrs. Jackson began weighing the possibility that she was being attacked, she realized that she was seeing not a flesh-and-blood head, but its image in the polished panel above her head. She blotted it out with a pillow.

Later, while awaiting her turn to make her toilette in the ladies' dressing room, she learned that her expe-

rience was relatively mild. Another woman told of awakening to the consciousness of a soft, shifting, heavy weight upon her head. It turned out to be no harmless reflection, but the actual feet of an American gentleman which had somehow come through from the next bunk to join her in casual intimacy.

For the brave and patient, all things pass. Eventually the westering trains climbed the Sierra, threaded their way through the Summit Tunnel and crept along the dizzying shelf of Cape Horn, almost 2,000 feet above the thin, faraway thread of the American River. And, at length, the trains came down to the flower-decked town of Sacramento, where they stopped before the final leg of the journey to San Francisco was undertaken.

For some travelers, the arrival at San Francisco brought a new round of pleasure. Certainly it did for the excursion party that came from Boston in 1870. By special arrangement their train rolled down Market Street to stop directly before the Grand Hotel, and the passengers disembarked. During their stay they went down to the ocean beach, and there they mixed some water from the Pacific with a bottle of Atlantic water they had brought from Massachusetts Bay ("The union of these two waters," said their leader Alexander Rice, "seems typical of the commingling of a great people whose future should be one"). They were wined and dined at private estates, and one night several citizens of the place gave a ball for the excursionists at the Cosmopolitan Hotel at which more than 500 guests danced until four o'clock in the morning.

These were exceptional diversions, restricted to a favored few. But for all travelers there remained forever in the memory that moment when the long train ride ended. After the plains, the deserts, the trestles over terrifying canyons, it was a great experience, and almost every traveler tried in his way to give expression to it.

Robert Louis Stevenson described his arrival with lasting eloquence: "Few people have praised God more happily than I did. And thenceforward, down by Blue Cañon, Alta, Dutch Flat, and all the old mining camps, through a sea of mountain forests, dropping thousands of feet toward the far sea-level as we went, not I only, but all the passengers on board, threw off their sense of dirt and heat and weariness, and bawled like school-boys, and thronged with shining eyes upon the platform and became new creatures within and without."

Safaris on wheels in the wilderness

Though their real purpose was moving people and freight over long distances, Western railroads were soon pressed into service as vehicles of pure pleasure. In this role, they helped to transform a forbidding frontier into a new playground, where hunting, fishing, picnicking and even mountain climbing could be enjoyed with ease and comfort.

Perhaps the most extravagant manifestation of the phenomenon was the use of private cars as mobile hunting lodges. The tracks led through land where wild fowl darkened the sky. Elk, antelope and blacktail deer frolicked on the prairie. Bear roamed the mountains and trout crowded the streams. And from a private car, rich Eastern sporting types could bag all this game while roughing it luxuriously.

One of the earliest of such cars (*below*) was taken westward by Jerome Marble, a Massachusetts manufacturer. Besides all the comforts of home, the car had gun racks, ammunition lockers and an icebox for preserving trophies of the hunt. In 1876, Marble, a friend and their families went on a safari to Dakota over the tracks of the unfinished Northern Pacific. They had such fun that, on returning home, Marble set up a company to build and rent private cars of all sorts for wealthy patrons.

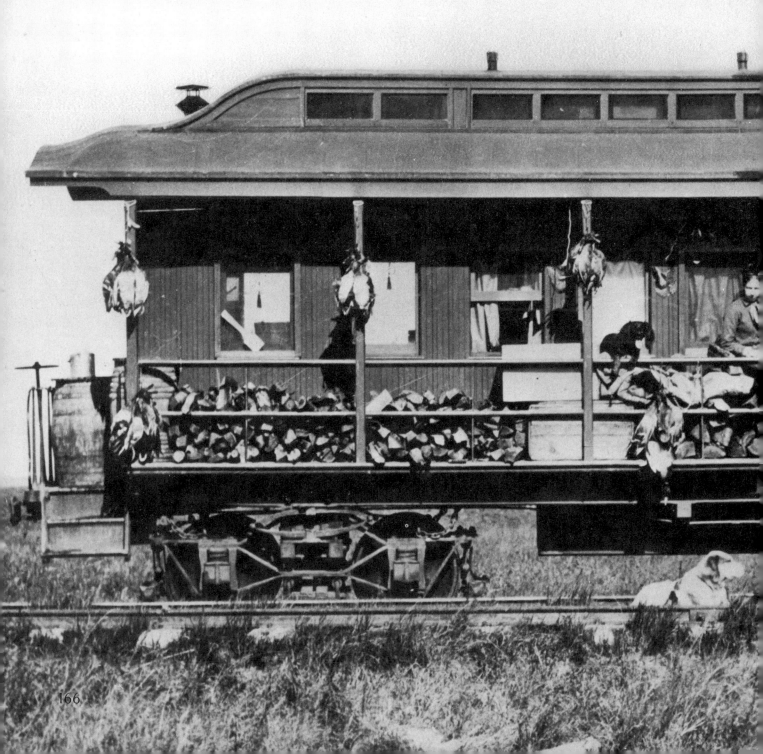

Sportsmen Jerome Marble and Henry Houghton, correctly garbed and with shotguns in hand, proudly stand before Marble's private hunting car on the Dakota prairie. Their wives, children and a guest line the car's long observation porch, behind hunting prizes that attest to their prowess.

Picnics by rail became a California fashion when short lines were built into the redwoods. In front of the North Pacific Coast's engine *Olema,* Bohemian Club members gather in newly accessible Elim Grove. Elim, mile spelled in reverse, indicates the park is exactly one mile from track's end.

5 | The men who made the trains go

Railroaders, to themselves, to all small boys and to most grownups were a breed apart from all other, lesser mortals. They traveled far and fast. They controlled immensely powerful devices. They lived dangerously: during a single month in 1887, 34 railroaders died on the job. Yet railroaders scorned other livelihoods, for railroading was the great adventure of the age.

The trainmen were part of a fraternity whose members worked their way up the ladder and were proud of their professional skills. Typically, the engineer started as a wiper, who swabbed caked oil from locomotives back from long trips; the lordly passenger-train conductor began as a brakeman teetering atop a freight car. United by shared pride in their jobs and perils, railroad men felt a deep sense of brotherhood.

A C.P. freight crew in 1883 consists of two brakemen (*far left and right*), conductor, engineer and fireman with mascot.

172

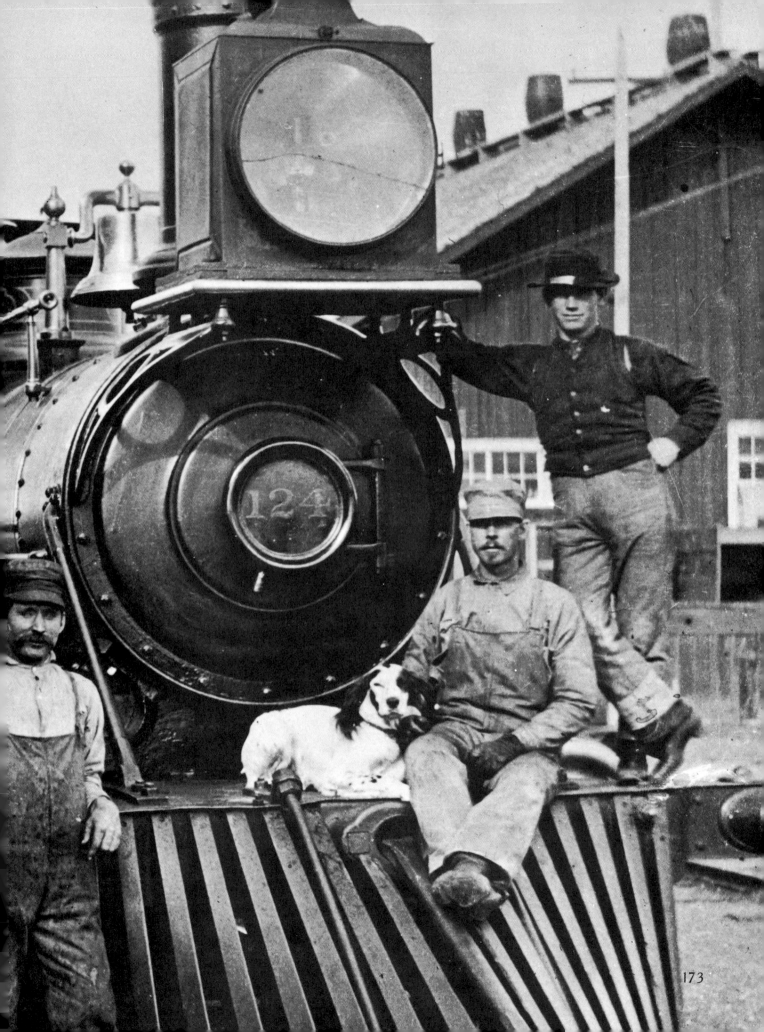

173

Members of a lifelong brotherhood

Most of the men who worked for the railroads of the Old West saw their first trains when young and, at the sight, let their breathless hearts tell them what to do with the rest of their lives. What they saw and heard—smoke and cinders belching from a diamond-shaped stack, the imperious screech of a locomotive whistle, the steamy cough of exhaust from a brass-bound behemoth—created a vision of unimaginable distances conquered by unimaginable power. At once they coveted its badges of honor: a striped cap, a red bandanna around the neck.

Some won those badges as pioneer railroaders west of the Missouri River, and never earned a living any other way, or wanted to. In the end they would all admit—or rather would brag, with a cross-grained pride in hardship—that their youthful vision had left out a lot. They were semihomeless (a man never knows Monday morning where he will be Wednesday midnight, ran the saying), almost comfortless, plagued by danger and unspeakable hours, hostage to all the caprices of nature and the rigid whims of the division superintendent.

Yet the railroaders followed that life, and followed it proudly. Two of these men, Henry Clay French and J. Harvey Reed, left records of their careers so detailed that they illuminate all of Western railroading from the 1870s to the 1890s. Henry French held just about every kind of job there was to be had: telegrapher, switchman, brakeman, baggageman, fireman, station agent, yardman, conductor. He was an engineer long enough to survive one wreck, and then, finding that he

disliked the job, quit. By contrast, Harvey Reed spent 40 years as an engineer.

The decades through which these two men railroaded embraced the whole history of railroad development in the West. They saw it all, endured it all, savored it all—tornadoes in Nebraska, the twisted canyons of the Rio Grande, the blizzards of Montana, the dizzy switchback up the spine of the Cascades, the snows of the Sierra, the deserts of Utah and Nevada, the Texas cattle with such a spread of horn that their heads had to be twisted cater-cornered to get them into a boxcar, the Indians, the gunslingers, the fires, the washouts, the falling bridges, the runaway trains, the wrecks—always the wrecks. From the Missouri to Puget Sound, from above the Canadian border to below the Mexican, their place of work was roughly 2,000 miles square. They railroaded when railroading, and everything else in the rambunctious West was like nothing anywhere else in the tamed world.

In 1888, the first year in which anybody thought to compile such statistics, 2,070 railroad men were killed in action, 20,148 were injured. When Henry Clay French got a job as a switchman in 1875, his older sister immediately set aside a clean white sheet for the disposal of his remains. She was not alone in her apprehension. Herbert Hamblen, another railroad man of the period, recalled that when he hired out as a switchman and was eager to go to work, the yardmaster told him, "Get your dinner first. There's no use of your getting killed on an empty stomach."

French and Reed began their careers with primitive equipment almost totally unfit for the job of coping with the distances, the hazards and the terrain of the West. The best locomotives of the early 1870s topped out around 35 tons, blew up on whim and did well to exceed 35 miles an hour. Trains were likely to break into two or three chunks and career off the rails in sev-

After a fireman was killed in a wreck and his friends had to pass the hat for his widow's sake, the Brotherhood of Locomotive Firemen was formed in 1873. The commemorative poster (left) illustrated the way in which members could help each other.

The glamor of a railroad assignment made railway mail clerks the aristocrats of the postal service. For sorting letters on speeding trains they got extra pay and the additional rewards of travel and excitement.

eral directions. On a downgrade, engineers did not rely on brakes alone; they also wrestled with a cranky, four-foot reverse lever called a Johnson bar and spun fire from driving wheels in an effort to keep everything from falling off the mountain—and did not always succeed. The roadbeds over which they ran had often been laid down in careless haste, trestles wobbled on their timber knees, and nature compounded their difficulties. (It was still possible, for instance, for a brakeman to get chased by an ill-tempered bear.)

Before Reed and French finally hung up their caps and coveralls, they were running locomotives that weighed close to 50 tons and could run at more than 50 miles an hour on a clear track. By the end of the 1880s their trains were equipped with reliable, efficient Westinghouse air brakes—which had been invented and put to use in the East 15 years earlier. And at long last, the automatic coupler and air brakes, both of which saved human lives, were made mandatory by a federal statute passed in 1893.

So, having survived to retirement, both French and Reed were able to set down detailed recollections of their perilous work. French, who left a fuller record of his thoughts, made it clear that he considered himself a full-fledged railroader in 1875, when he was almost 16 years old. He had been a very young orphan when he saw his first train, and the sight should have—but did not—scare him off for good. In Sumner, Illinois, he watched a brakeman fall to his death between two flatcars, and walked off convinced that he himself would never be guilty of such clumsiness were he fortunate enough to become a railroad man. French saw his sec-

To freight crews, the caboose was for days
at a time office, storeroom and the equiv-
alent of a ship's fo'c'sle, where they ate and
slept. This intimacy bred the mutual trust
needed for safe and efficient operations.

ond train in 1873, when he was 13; by that time he had been bound out to work as a farmhand, but he tied the team he was driving to a hitching rail, ran to the depot and stowed away on the train.

He got his first railroad job that same year, as a messenger. With the help of a sympathetic older man, he learned the Morse code and, at the age of 14, he was working as a full-time railroad telegrapher. Two years of that job gave him all he wanted of the sedentary life —and so he applied for and got the switchman's job that so alarmed his sister. In the yard French soon came under the tutelage of an old hand named Jack Foster, who undertook to teach him the tricks of dealing with link-and-pin couplings.

The link was an iron hoop 13 inches long, exactly like a single link of a huge chain. To stitch a train to-

gether, a switchman pushed one end of a link into a slot in the iron drawbar of a car, and fastened it with a big iron spike (the pin) thrust through a hole in the drawbar; the other end of the link and another pin went into the drawbar of the other car being coupled.

But the operation was not as simple as it seems. When a link was disengaged from one car, it dropped from the end of the other at an angle of about 30°. To get at it, the switchman stepped between the cars—or ran between them if they were moving—lifted the hanging link in his hand and guided it into the drawbar of the next car. In theory, the link could be guided with a brakeman's club, a hickory staff about three feet long, known scornfully as the staff of ignorance. But old hands knew they would be laughed at if they were seen using the thing, so they did not—and it was said around the

Section gangs, like this Chicago, Burlington & Quincy crew, rode the rails on handcars to replace rotted ties, tamp loose spikes and tighten bolts. As a memento of their shared sense of responsibility, they struck this pose in the 1870s. Their foreman's solemn little daughter is in a place of honor.

For every conductor or ticket clerk a passenger saw, dozens of other men worked behind the scenes to keep the trains running. Here a Union Pacific crew turns out with its varied tools in the Omaha railyard.

yards in those days that the way to tell a switchman was to look for missing fingers.

A switchman risked his life as well as his fingers. The drawbars of any two cars often were set at different heights above the roadbed, and so were the heavy beams that served as bumpers between cars. To overcome such discrepancies, bent links known as gooseneck links were provided, but many a switchman was crushed to death when one bumper beam slid over the other while he was between cars. The danger was compounded when a train was on the move and the switchman had to keep his feet clear of switching points and out from under rolling train wheels while concentrating his attention on the stubborn link-and-pin.

Few succeeded forever. French's mentor, Jack Foster, did not. French remembered the night scene in detail: "We were making up a train. A light haze of rain made everything slippery. I took the first car and, after some trouble with a pin that would not drop, succeeded in reaching in with another pin and beating it into place. Jack took his turn at the next coupling. One car's coupling slot was considerably higher than that of the other. Jack stepped over to the linkbox and selected a gooseneck link. He fitted it into the low car and cocked the pin on the high car. He signalled the engineer to back up. The two cars touched firmly, but the difference was so great that a coupling could not be made.

"Jack signalled the engineer to go ahead. As soon as the cars separated, Jack signalled the engineer to stop. With the lantern in the crook of his arm, Jack was working desperately to release the pin in the slot of the low car, but it would not free. Suddenly I noticed that the

cars were closer together, The rear section was moving. 'Jack!' I screamed, 'Slack running!' He heard me. A glance told him of his danger and he tried to spring clear. There was a split second when it seemed he would make it. I can shut my eyes yet and see the tiny slip of his foot. His body was caught between the cars as though in a giant vise."

Foster's death almost broke French's heart, but it did not break his nerve. He took a job braking on the Santa Fe's cattle runs to Dodge City. After the switch-yard, the job of brakeman offered certain compensations. Though he was known to his brethren by such half-contemptuous titles as "brakie" or "shack," French now got to board the rolling stock and ride the road, which seemed to him the only proper life for a rail-roader. In good weather, on a clear track, there were

few situations more pleasant than sitting atop a swaying boxcar, legs dangling, and watching the prairie go by with its scattered buffalo and Indians. Moreover, whether a brakie was married or lived in a railroad boarding-house, he soon learned that running on the road gave his larder the pick of the freshest eggs and vegetables and the ripest fruit, bought from farm wives who came to the way stations to sell their produce. And during a long run, life in a caboose — known to the profession as the crummy — could be agreeable.

Herbert Hamblen remembered one crummy with particular fondness: "We had a fine, big, eight-wheel ca-boose, right out of the paint shop, red outside and green inside. There were six bunks in her, a row of lockers on each side to sit on and keep supplies in, a stove and table, and a desk for the conductor. We furnished our

181

own bedding and cooking utensils, and we had a pleasant and comfortable home on wheels. As the boys had good taste, we soon had the car looking like a young lady's boudoir. We had lace curtains in front of the bunks, a mat the flagman had swiped from a sleeping car, a dog, and a canary."

The fact that Henry French now had a job he coveted did not mean that he led a life of unalloyed delight. The primitive hand brakes he had to operate were devil's devices that could be manipulated only by means of iron wheels located on the roofs of the cars. So the brakies (generally two to a train) rode up top in every kind of weather. They were there when the sun shone and a pleasant breeze cooled their skins, but they were also there when rain soaked their clothing and wind froze it to armor plate. When the engineer whistled for brakes, one brakie would start from the front end, and the other from the rear, and they would work toward one another, car by car. On a black night, with sleet icing the running boards that led along the tops of the cars, it was worth a man's life to gauge and jump the 30 inches between one bucking boxcar and the next.

At best, hand brakes were slow to take hold. On a downgrade they often let slack pile up unevenly along the length of a train, bringing on the embarrassment — or, all too often, the calamity — of a break-in-two. The even application of brakes throughout a train called for skill and long practice. Railroad owners devised a sobering punishment for a brakie who tightened down too hard, skidding and flattening wheels. The price of the wheels, usually about $45 apiece, was deducted from his paycheck — and at that time a brakeman's pay was exactly $45 a month.

Along with the problems of braking, there were difficulties encountered with the occasional passengers carried by French's freight trains. He generally liked the trail-driving cowboys who cared for the nervous, bawling steers in a cattle train; he considered cowpokes to be hard-working men, loyal to their calling and fully entitled to raise as much hell as they could manage after long months on the trail. The real problem involved with handling cattle, he felt, was that the cowboys rode along in the caboose. "We dreaded trips on cattle trains that included two different outfits," he later wrote. "On such trains the crews prudently stayed out of the caboose. Fights and gun fights started over insults, trivial

All spiffed up to meet the public, Union
Pacific employees stand behind the ticket
counter in Kansas City. Managed by
Thomas Shaw *(in top hat)*, this office
was one of the line's busiest and fanciest.

and often fancied. One such that left our caboose a total wreck started over a cowboy's remark, 'I don't like to play cards with a dirty deck.' One of the rival outfit had understood him to say, 'dirty neck.'"

When French was running in and out of the cattle town of Hunnewell, Kansas, he and the others of his crew learned to douse headlights, caboose running lights and even brakemen's lanterns after sundown, because cowboys would shoot at anything that glimmered in the night. One night French's brother Almond, having recently caught on as a brakeman, forgot this precaution —and his red lantern literally exploded in his hand. Nobody could find Almond the rest of that night, but he turned up next morning trudging along the tracks. Almond explained that he had spent a safe and restful night inside a culvert, two miles out of town. "For that shot to hit my lantern," he told his brother, "it had to go between my legs."

During his service in the cow country, French became a freight conductor, at least part of the time. Except for the paper work, his new post meant little change in his life, since freight conductors were expected to spell their brakies when the need arose. About the greatest eminence he derived from his role as a glorified brakeman was the satisfaction of seeing his own shaving mug, bearing his name in gold leaf, installed in a place of honor in a barber shop at Ottawa, Kansas.

French and his trains continued to encounter the West's peculiar hazards. Once a plague of grasshoppers blackened the sky, and those that were crushed by earlier trains so greased the rails that the locomotive pulling French's freight stalled until the tracks were shoveled clear. Another time, when his crew had a running contest with a herd of horses that insisted, foolishly, on pasturing directly on the right of way, the engine killed them off a few at a time and reclaimed a clear track. French also recorded an unscheduled stop on a bridge to cut down a horse thief who had been lynched on one of the girders. On another occasion he climbed to the top of the caboose while his train was underway and found a fellow with two guns sitting there. The man pointed one of the guns at French and suggested that the weapon's presence constituted his fare. While they debated the point, another trainman sneaked up behind the gunman and laid him out with the staff of ignorance—and afterward collected a $2,000 reward for the capture of the desperado, who, it turned out, was wanted for murder.

More than once French's knowledge of the Morse code drew him back to the job he detested. One day in 1876 his train pulled into Emporia, Kansas, for a dinner stop. French could not go off with the crew to eat because he was dead broke, having unwisely bet against a pat poker hand the night before. To take his mind off his stomach, he went to the telegraph office. When the telegrapher's bug began to chatter, French's brain automatically registered the message, an order for his train to "meet an extra" at the next station—that is, to pull off on a siding while an unscheduled train went by. French rejoined his train, assuming that the conductor would take the order from the telegrapher as a matter of routine. But when the conductor highballed them through the next station, he felt a sudden sickening dread, went over the boxcars and asked the boss whether he hadn't received the order. "My God!" yelled the conductor, "I forgot to get my orders. Stop the train!" They braked in frantic haste and took the sidetrack just in time for the extra to pound by.

French had to confess how he happened to know about the order and was instantly promoted to the post of brakeman-operator, with the added duty of taking and relaying orders now and then. It was not the last time he returned to the telegraph. There was a day in Washington State when, running as a conductor, he found the operator in a one-man station at his key dead of a heart attack. Again French betrayed himself by tapping out this intelligence to the dispatcher—and was appointed to fill the dead man's shoes temporarily. Still later in Oregon, while waiting for a job on the rolling stock, he agreed to work as night operator. When he found that he couldn't stand being cooped up he tried to resign. Operators were in short supply that year and his superiors, counting on French's respect for the telegrapher's trust, simply ignored his resignation messages. Finally, in indignation, French took matters into his own hands. He pulled the plugs on his telegraph lines, hid the keys and went to the Umatilla House hotel to play poker and get drunk. After several hours two passenger trains and three freights were stalled for lack of orders, and his resignation was accepted.

As a station agent, a job that in smaller depots usually went along automatically with the telegrapher's post, French learned to sell tickets, handle baggage and answer questions. Like other agent-operators at small stations throughout the West, he discovered that the job's primary requirement was learning the art of killing time while being lonely. One of his contemporaries, Clarence Wooster, who worked as an agent at the Central Pacific station at Auburn in the Sierra foothills, recalled that the high points of his day came just before the arrival of the up-train in the morning and the down-train in the afternoon, when his station platform turned into a boardwalk for display of the town's newest hats, gowns and parasols. People who came to watch trains arrive and depart—and they included most of the able-bodied population of Auburn—invariably asked how each train was running that day. Usually Wooster had to answer, "She's twenty minutes late," which always elicited the same sophisticated comment about a piece of car-coupling equipment that was forever breaking down: "Guess she pulled a drawhead again. They ought to do something about them drawheads." When Wooster wearied of answering the question, he tried putting up a permanent sign that "she" would be 20 minutes late. It worked only partially; everybody now asked him whether the sign referred to *today's* train.

Now and again, in early days on the Western plains, the station agent's boredom was compounded with peril. Cy Warman, a railroad historian of the period, recorded an incident on the Union Pacific in the early '70s at a Nebraska whistle stop called Wood River. The only permanent residents were a settler named Bankers, his wife, his infant daughter, a young schoolteacher named Emma, who presided over a one-room schoolhouse for the children in the surrounding country-side, and an unnamed station agent-operator. The operator's shack contained no more than a telegraph key, a stove, his bed and an iron safe, but it had double-board walls with four inches of sand between them to keep out the winter's chill.

When a passing Pawnee warned of a Sioux war party in the area, the agent informed the Bankerses, and then tapped out a message to Ogallala, 165 miles to the west. Knowing that their cabin and the station would be likely targets, the Bankerses and the teacher took refuge in a cattle car on the siding, but the agent refused to join them; he had to stay with his key. The war party struck after dark, set fire to the Bankerses'

cabin and attacked the station. The baby was sick with colic and the adults were in deadly fear that her crying would attract the Sioux. But for the time being, the war party was fully occupied in their attack upon the agent, who valiantly fought back from his well-armored station. Eventually, Mrs. Bankers succeeded in soothing her baby with 20 drops of paregoric—though she was terrified that the heavy dose would kill the infant.

One warrior climbed into the car. Desperately aware of the need for silence, Bankers killed him with his clubbed rifle. Soon afterward the station agent, fighting from behind his iron safe, had one leg shattered by a Sioux bullet. And then, when the battle seemed all but lost, a relief train, running without lights, arrived with a party of Army officers and Pawnee scouts and routed the Sioux. To complete the storybook ending, the conductor of that train later married the schoolteacher.

Happily, Henry French never faced such an adventure. Instead, he climbed smoothly up the ladder from station agent to conductor. In a train crew, particularly on a passenger run, the conductor held the post of ultimate dignity. He was the captain of the train, and his job demanded a fine sense of diplomacy, beginning with the traditional chore of dealing politely with a woman who could not see why she should pay half fare for her "ten-year-old" son—even though the boy was sprouting whiskers. Conductors had to handle crooked gamblers (some conductors discreetly slipped warning cards to passengers who seemed about to be lured into a game of faro, three-card monte or poker) and to argue gently against the wisdom of firing pistols out the window at passing telegraph poles.

These were everyday problems. The real excitement of the job stemmed from the emergencies. On one trip French delivered a baby, cutting the umbilical cord with the same knife he used to carve his plug of chewing tobacco. Another time, defying all the regulations against carrying victims of infectious diseases, he took aboard a girl desperately ill with scarlet fever and took her 40 miles to Albina, where she could get medical attention. Once a Chinese laborer, his fingers horribly smashed in a bridge-building accident, was put aboard his train. French got the man drunk on three tumblers of whiskey; then he carefully splinted the hand and poulticed it with some vaseline and a cud of well-chewed tobacco. "The severed finger healed perfectly." he reported. ◉

A clannish and all-pervasive way of life

Railroading was an all-encompassing way of life; even when off duty, railroad men spent their spare time with fellow railroaders. Firemen, conductors, engineers and even mighty division superintendents often had their houses on the Railroad Avenue that was found in nearly every town served by the train company. Railroaders played baseball against other railroad teams. They tooted their horns in company bands that made their appearances at local and statewide celebrations. They formed their own volunteer fire companies — putting their own money down to pay for the uniforms — and fought only railroad fires. Railroad workers' loyalty reflected the paternalism of the companies. And whole communities basked in the glory of being a divisional headquarters or the site of repair shops.

This 1891 baseball team brought glory to the Yakima & Pacific Coast line.

Every member of the Colorado Midland Railway's prize-winning band except the director, M. O. Barnes *(foreground)* was a full-time

The Union Pacific's Durant Engine and Hose Company, a volunteer fire company, railroaders all, was formed in 1871 at Omaha.

railroader. But even Barnes, a professional who led the Colorado Springs Opera House orchestra for 26 years, was on the railroad's payroll.

Braced against a Western blizzard, the brakeman in this romanticized drawing struggles to bring a freight to an emergency stop. To hand-brake the five cars in his care, he had to jump from roof to icy roof.

The job in sharpest contrast to the conductor's post of all-round diplomat and medical miracle worker was held by the fireman—and Henry French filled that job, too. Like many a railroad man, he coveted the fireman's title of "tallow pot," since it was only through service as a black, greasy fireman that he could move on to become that lordly being, an engineer. The name tallow pot came from one of a fireman's more terrifying duties. Whenever an engineer felt that the sliding valves above a locomotive's big steam cylinders needed oiling, the fireman took a long-spouted can of liquid tallow, climbed out on the running boards of the speeding locomotive, crept alongside the hot boiler and poured the tallow on the valves. (The duty ended in the 1880s, when most locomotives were fitted with a device that mixed oil with the boiler water, thus creating steam that carried its own lubricant.)

No American ever worked harder for $2.40 a day than a fireman on the Western railroads. Early engines burned anywhere from 40 to 200 pounds of coal per mile, depending partly on the grade and the quality of the fuel, but mostly on the engineer. On occasion —swinging his body, his shovel and the firebox door like a complex triple pendulum—a fireman might move more than two tons of coal in less than half an hour. And keeping a fire hot by spreading coal through the firebox, from front to back and into the corners, called for skill of a high order along with mere brute strength.

A malicious or incompetent engineer, sitting on "the four-dollar side of the cab," could make the job a lot harder for the man on the $2.40 side. Herbert Hamblen found that out early. There were two ways to run an engine, he learned. One way was to nurse the locomotive, keeping consumption of fuel and water to a minimum. The other consisted of "pounding" her and pouring the coal out the stack. After working with an engineer who always liked to have lots of coal, Hamblen drew a relief engineer of another school. Hamblen bent his back as usual until the engineer stopped him. "Is there somebody buried back there, an' you're trying to dig him out?" the engineer asked sardonically. "Get up there on your seat an' sit down! You've got enough coal in there to run to the next water plug right now, so crack your door an' let's have a smoke."

One of the heaviest burdens on a fireman's life was moral rather than physical. According to the unwritten railroad code, he had to wait for a signal from his engineer before he could jump out of a locomotive that was in danger of being wrecked. Considering the variety of circumstances under which that act became advisable, it must have been extraordinarily difficult to accept somebody else's judgment in the matter. Engine crews went over the side because of head-end or rear-end collisions, break-in-twos, runaway cars, crumbling bridges, washouts, boulders or trees across the tracks, broken or missing rails or any of a dozen other unforeseeable crises. Of course, the burden might have been even heavier on the engineer. It was up to him to make the decision to jump or ride it out.

Henry French had to make that decision just once during his brief career in the four-dollar seat. The incident took place at a mountaintop construction site where French was running his engine and a single flatcar. As he started downgrade with a load of construction material, his brakeman, a powerful fellow named Smith, tightened the flatcar brake so much that the brake chain broke and the backlash spun him around in a circle. The train began to pick up momentum; French threw the Johnson bar into reverse, but still she went. Recovering from his sudden spin, Smith tried to slow the juggernaut with the brake on the locomotive's tender —and broke that chain as well.

"Unload!" French yelled at the crew, and they immediately leaped from the train. A moment later, with the scenery going past him in a blur, he clambered down the steps of his cab, crouched as low as he could, said a small prayer and let go. When he finally stopped tumbling and got to his feet, he could see the last sign of his train —a cloud of smoke and steam in a ditch far down the mountainside. As far as French was concerned, one such experience was more than enough. He limped uphill to the construction site, borrowed the telegraph key and sent in his resignation on the spot.

The locomotive engineer of those days, particularly in the West, was a hero—and, like a hero of antiquity, he enjoyed perquisites of office envied by lesser men. He could have his engine painted in any grand color scheme that suited his artistic instincts: yellow wheels, blue stack, the brassworks shined as bright as he fancied, a red cab with his locomotive's name and number painted in gold and set off in arabesque curlicues. He could and did convert his whistle into a personal mu-

sical instrument, altering its tone with wooden plugs until its voice was unmistakably his own. Pulling into his home station, he usually sounded a special toot to advise wife or landlady that it was time to put supper on the table.

But an engineer did not reach his lofty estate simply by aspiring to it. Cy Warman described a painful apprenticeship. An aspiring young man began as a wiper, working a 12-hour shift in the roundhouse, where he massaged the internal parts of some engineer's beloved locomotive with wads of greasy waste. The pay was $1.75 a day. A wiper could become an engine watchman, whose job it was to keep water in the boiler and enough of a fire going to move the locomotive within the railroad yard. From there, he could move up to switch-engine fireman, road fireman and hostler, which meant going into the yard, picking up an engine where an engineer had left her and running her into the roundhouse. The final steps were switch-engine engineer and—at last—journeyman "hogger," a real live locomotive engineer. "A great advantage the men of the West had was that they served as a rule less than three years as firemen," wrote Cy Warman.

J. Harvey Reed must have broken most of the records for advancement, even for the West. He became an engineer within three years of his first job as a fireman. But he had been a railroad buff long before then. In 1852, when he was five years old, a construction train came grumbling alongside his father's farm in Pennsylvania to lay the first rails he ever saw. The sight of rails and rolling stock filled him with a mixture of terror and worshipful awe—and his feelings were reinforced when the railroad built a station a mile away and named it Reed. He left the farm at 20; less than a year later he caught on with a Midwestern road as a rookie fireman. Then, in 1871, he started his career of four decades as an engineer west of the Missouri. At one time or another during those 40 years, Harvey Reed worked on the Santa Fe, the Oregon Railroad and Navigation, the Northern Pacific, the Great Northern, the Fort

Worth and Rio Grande, and the Mexican National Railroad.

It was not all a straight run on a clear track. For one thing, Reed hated the perverse way in which frail humans insisted on obstructing the rails with their bodies. An engineer's lurking anguish lay in the fact that he knew, better than any soul alive, how much track it took to stop a hurtling locomotive—as much as 3,000 feet for a 50-car, hand-braked train going at 40 miles an hour. The horror was that he could rarely catch sight of anything as small as a human being in time.

Reed was at the throttle when two women were killed on a bridge, and took what comfort he could from the last words spoken by one of them: "Don't blame the engineer." But he also had miraculous luck. Once he spied a drunk sleeping it off between the rails, and stopped in time to pull the man out from under the cowcatcher, comatose but whole. On another bridge a nine-year-old girl, seeing the juggernaut upon her, threw herself down upon the ties just outside the rails. She survived nearly the full length of the train, but then she reared up slightly and was brushed off the bridge and into the creek below by the steps of the last car. Reed saw her fall, dove into the water and rescued her.

The most improbable near miss of all came when Reed and his engine got into trouble on the Stampede switchback in the Cascades. The switchback, a series of three graduated runs up the side of the mountain, served as a makeshift route during the boring of the great Stampede Tunnel (page 104). Driving No. 457, a 10-wheel Baldwin locomotive, Reed brought a trainload of bridge timbers to the foot of the switchback and started up the slope. "Up we crawled at a snail's pace, the engine working every ounce of power she possessed, until we struck some freshly laid rails and she no sooner struck these—possibly covered with grease—than she went off her feet like a fat lady encountering a banana peeling on a sidewalk. God! How I sweat trying to coax that engine to her feet before I felt her slipping hopelessly under me." Soon all forward motion

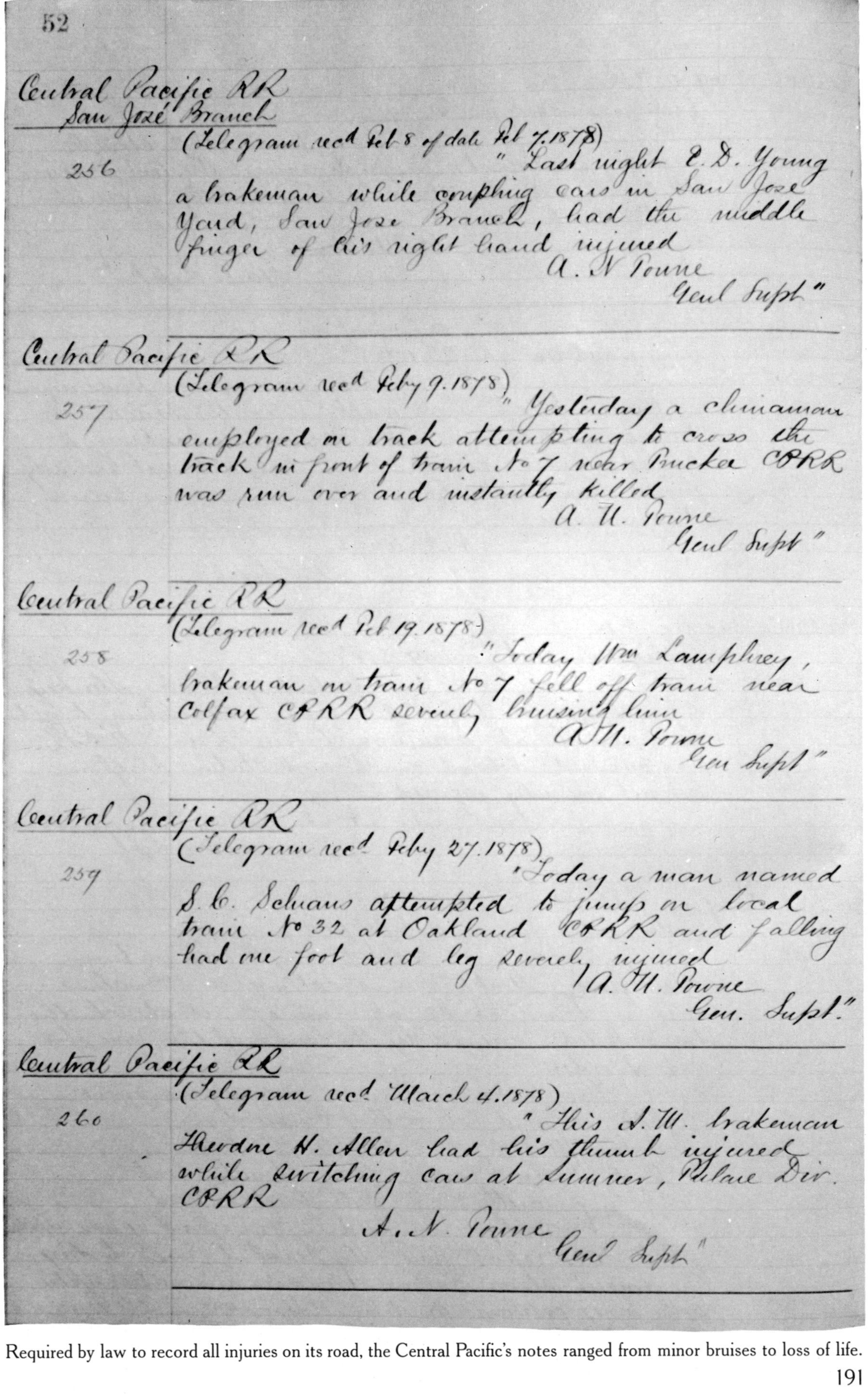

Central Pacific RR
San José Branch

256
(Telegram rec'd Feb 8 of date Feb 7, 1878)
"Last night E. D. Young
a brakeman while coupling cars in San Jose
Yard, San Jose Branch, had the middle
finger of his right hand injured
A. N. Towne
Genl Supt"

Central Pacific RR

257
(Telegram rec'd Feby 9, 1878) "Yesterday a chinaman
employed on track attempting to cross the
track in front of train No 7 near Bucka CPRR
was run over and instantly killed
A. N. Towne
Genl Supt"

Central Pacific RR

258
(Telegram rec'd Feb 19, 1878)
"Today Wm Lamphrey,
brakeman on train No 7 fell off train near
Colfax CPRR severely bruising him
A N. Towne
Gen Supt"

Central Pacific RR

259
(Telegram rec'd Feby 27, 1878)
"Today a man named
S. C. Schaus attempted to jump on local
train No 32 at Oakland CPRR and falling
had one foot and leg severely injured
A. N. Towne
Gen. Supt."

Central Pacific RR

260
(Telegram rec'd March 4, 1878)
"His S. M. brakeman
Theodore H. Allen had his thumb injured
while switching cars at Summer, Palace Div.
CPRR
A. N. Towne
Genl Supt"

Required by law to record all injuries on its road, the Central Pacific's notes ranged from minor bruises to loss of life.

C.B.HUTCHINS PATENT

192

Railroad officials clamber over a tangled mound of iron and steel—the grim result of a head-on collision between two Central Pacific trains near Truckee, California. Such calamities, in which six times as many railroad workers as passengers died each year, were frequent on the single-track Western lines with their rudimentary signaling systems.

ceased, and they began to slide backward down the mountain. "I realized she was beyond all control and turned to the fireman to tell him to jump, but he had already gone and I followed, landing in a snowbank."

A mile down the track and 330 feet lower on the slope, a construction worker named One-Eyed Jerry Simpson sat astride a tie on a trestle, hauling up a timber from the gorge 90 feet below him. He saw 457 coming, and as he watched, the loaded flatcars broke loose and careened off into the ravine. But that brought little solace to One-Eyed Jerry; the runaway locomotive was still bearing down upon him and it was 200 feet to either end of the trestle. In despair he threw himself across the left rail to get it over with quickly. By now, No. 457 was swaying wildly, nearly losing her grip on the rails. Then, just before she reached Simpson, 457 heeled up on her right-hand wheels — and the left drivers, pilot wheels and tender trucks passed above Simpson's body with daylight to spare.

At the best of times, from an engineer's point of view, mountain work was unrelievedly dangerous. Among the worst of the perils was the tendency of his fragile link-and-pin couplings to snap. On a downgrade, the engineer had to keep what cars he had left racing ahead of the pursuing free-running section — and on a steep grade, free-running cars were likely to coast faster than any engine could run and still hold the rails. Once when Herbert Hamblen was pulling a heavy mixed freight, his train broke apart in a tunnel. Before him lay a seven-mile downhill run past two stations, and at each station a train would be switching on or off the main track. Hamblen knew he was in for trouble. Peering to his rear, he saw the loose cars "shoot out of the tunnel like a comet." Just out of the tunnel the track took a curve, and Hamblen was horrified to see the light, four-wheeled caboose flip off the tracks and drop 500 feet into a river, carrying his conductor and both of his brakemen. Now there was no one left to control the runaway section. Hamblen yelled at his fireman to jump, but by then the engine was gyrating so wildly that coal was pouring into the cab and out to the roadbed. A moment later the fireman himself was flung out of the cab to his death.

Hamblen desperately began to blow the broke-in-two signal — four long blasts, repeated again and again. He fully expected that the switch at the first station would

The great Crush crash

As if the real perils of railroading were not harrowing enough, at least one line deliberately staged a disaster as a public show. William George Crush, general passenger agent of the Missouri-Kansas-Texas (nicknamed the Katy) line, had seen the way train wrecks drew instant crowds. Early in 1896 he convinced the Katy's management that the line could make money by hauling people to see a planned collision. For months he plastered Katy territory with circus-style posters trumpeting the unparalleled spectacle of two trains meeting head-on at top speed. His co-stars were two aging locomotives gaudily repainted red and green. Newspapers ran yards of copy on Crush's crash.

On September 15 about 40,000 spectators, most of them brought by M-K-T excursion trains, thronged the temporary tent city of Crush, Texas, alongside the Katy tracks between Waco and Hillsboro. They munched fried chicken from picnic baskets or ate in a restaurant under a circus tent that Crush had provided along with five Katy tank cars of drinking water.

It took the 200 deputy sheriffs Crush had recruited some hours to push back the crowds to an apparently safe distance from the sign reading "Point of Collision." Finally the two locomotives, each pulling six coaches loaded with ties and covered with posters advertising a fair at Dallas and a circus at Waco, chugged toward each other. They touched cowcatchers in ceremonial salute, then each backed up a mile or so and stood, panting. Crush waved his sun helmet, the two crews leaped to safety and the trains lunged forward, whistles shrieking, throttles lashed wide open.

Fireworks signals rattled on the rails like musketry as the trains hurtled toward each other at 60 miles an hour. The engines crashed, reared up like fighting lions, then fell sideways.

But even Crush had not anticipated the tragic anticlimax. Both locomotive boilers exploded. A barrage of wood and metal sprayed the landscape, miraculously killing only two spectators and injuring a few others. The crowd succored the victims, gathered souvenirs and went home to treasure the memory of the biggest man-made disaster they were ever likely to see.

A flying bolt felled photographer J. C. Deane as he snapped this picture of the colliding trains. He lived to be known as Joe One-Eye Deane.

After the crash, spectators swarmed over the wrecked locomotives and surviving coaches, picking up grisly mementos of the spectacular event.

be closed, hurling him into a sidetracked train. But an alert flagman heard the shrieks of the whistle and threw the switch in time for Hamblen to rocket through a station at which he should have been going dead slow. Seeing the juggernaut hurtle past, the telegrapher wired the station below, where a three-car passenger local was making a stop. If those cars were on the main line, Hamblen would kill everybody aboard. He thundered through the station; the passenger train was on a siding, its occupants staring at him goggle-eyed.

Beyond the station, a man at the switch to another sidetrack gave him a highball signal by waving a lantern in a high semicircle. Hamblen roared through on the main track. Immediately the man threw the switch and the runaway cars swerved into the siding, ramming a line of coal cars and leaving both tracks blockaded with a devil's nest of rails, flour and machinery. Hamblen stopped and counted his casualties—four dead.

Now and again an engineer had an instant to choose between his own life and the lives of others. The moment came for Harvey Reed one day when he was pulling a 10-car passenger train near Buckley, Washington. Reed was speeding up to 40 miles an hour after slowly negotiating a stretch of new track around a great bulge in a mountainside. Suddenly, three car lengths ahead, he saw that one full rail was missing from the track—re-

Like horsemen showing off a stable of winning thoroughbreds, the crew of Kansas Pacific Roundhouse No. 8 at Armstrong, Kansas, assembles in

moved, presumably, by train robbers in the hope of causing a lootable wreck. Almost instinctively, Reed realized that he could save his passengers' lives by breaking the train in two; the Pullmans and coaches might stop in time, even though his engine was doomed.

He hit the emergency brake, then jammed the throttle all the way ahead, and the train did break. Two Pullmans at the back stopped almost at once; four coaches rolled 40 feet to a gentle stop—on the rails. The engine, a mail car, a baggage car and an empty coach plunged into the gap and toppled 250 feet down the mountainside. With them went Reed, his fireman, a mail clerk, a baggageman and one of the two brakemen on the train. Nothing much was left of the rolling stock—but against all reason, the five men were alive.

After such catastrophes, it was almost a relief to face the ordinary problems of an engineer's profession. One of those problems was snow—and snow could be merciless, whether it fell among the cuts of the Central Pacific in the Sierra, on the wind-tortured plains of Montana or amid the peaks of the Cascades.

In the mid-1880s, Cy Warman rode an engine into the Sierra to add more power to a snowplow. Up there, as many as a dozen engines would sometimes push a plow weighted with 25 tons of pig iron against 18-foot drifts. But the engine Cy was riding never did

1873 beside the engines in its charge. Roundhouse men kept their locomotives in constant readiness to replace any that met trouble on the road.

Engineer Bart Casey *(far right)* so loved the Oregon & California's No. 1361 that he paid to nickel-plate its fittings and redo its cab with cushions, mirrors and a clock for himself and fireman Fred Beard *(left)*.

get to its rendezvous. On a short stretch of track, the crew kept up steam and listened to the echoing blasts of the big plow's whistle far up the mountain, and the bleat of a light engine stuck somewhere in between. When they hit their own drifts, the engine would come to a shuddering, bolt-loosening halt, buried in snow to the top of the stack. From the top of the mountain it took the big plow seven days to reach them, and when she hit the last drift on the downslope she bore straight through it, creating a neatly roofed tunnel all her own.

At least there were snowplows in the area. Toward the end of his career, when he was in western Montana for the Great Northern, Harvey Reed bucked snow using only his engine's cowcatcher; not a single plow was available anywhere on his side of the drifts. "We would get up the track about a mile from the cut," he recalled. "We would then pull the throttle wide open and away we would go, kerchug into the wall of snow. The impact would drive the engine two or three car lengths into the drift, fastened into the grip of the snow so fast it would be necessary for the section crew to clear the snow out from our rear before we could get out and renew the attack. We fought and fought for 84 hours, without sleep and with only three meals in the whole period. After our 84 hours we reached Blackfoot, where we fed our faces. My fireman and I hit the hay and we slept for fifteen hours without batting an eye."

Yet Reed loved it all. His ordeal in the snow left behind it a proud memory of tenacity and strength of purpose. And for every such memory there was another of sheer delight. Here he is, in old age, looking back upon a night when he highballed along the Northern Pacific tracks in central Washington: "The moonlight was shining on the rails, giving them the appearance of silver threads reaching out across the barren plain. The 'old girl,' as we pulled out of Yakima, was prancing and champing at the bit, everything behind was snug, the track was clear, and all we had to do was go—and we surely went. Telegraph poles looked like they were planted only two feet apart, and the country appeared from the cab window like a rapidly moving panorama. Approaching the little stations there was a scream from the whistle, the clatter of a switch crossing, the blear of a depot, and on into the glimmer of the night."

For a Western railroad man, the poetry, power and speed of a night like that justified a lifetime of labor.

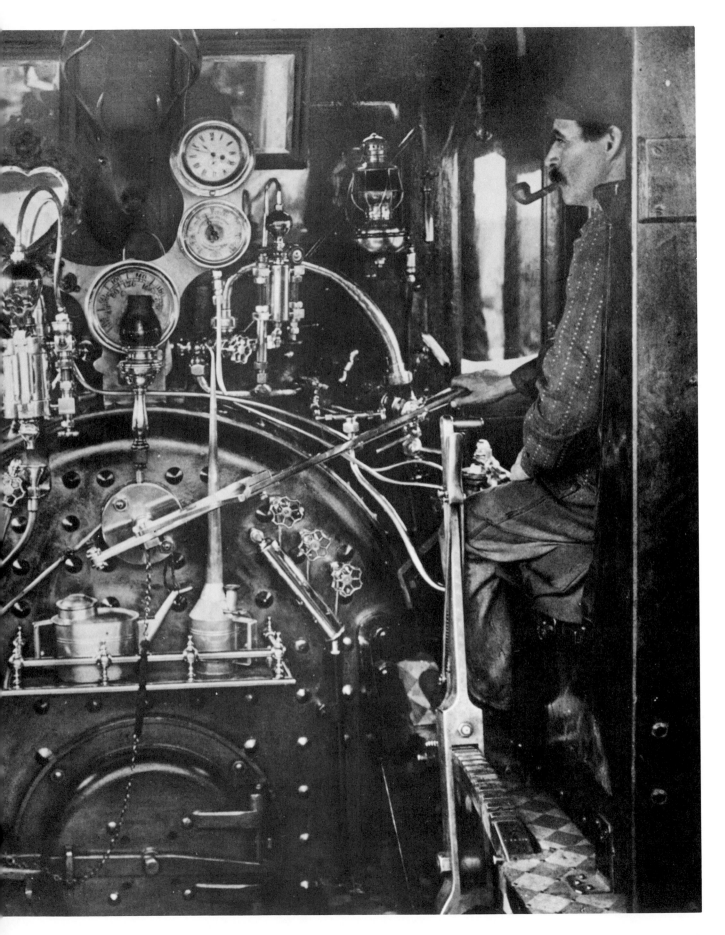

6 | A gaudy rail-borne harvest

During the last half of the 1860s, railroad crews laying track across the open Western plains paused every few miles to build a siding and a one-room station. They then gave the spot a name, which established it as the site of a future town. (Java, South Dakota, was named in honor of the good coffee served at a cookshack.) A decade later train passengers traveling through rich areas of the country looked out upon neatly patterned farming communities.

The railroads had brought people to the plains, enticing them with offers of cheap land—of which they had plenty to sell: railroads in Kansas controlled about one sixth of the state's territory. The people, in turn, were making the wilderness bloom with produce that was carried to market by rail.

It was the beginning of a rich collaboration, whose fruit is being celebrated in the picture below. The year was 1880, the place Atchison, Kansas. As

the town's brand-new station was dedicated, *Little Buttercup,* the Santa Fe's 4-4-0 engine, named for the appealing character of Gilbert and Sullivan's operetta *H.M.S. Pinafore,* stood laden with bounty harvested from the fertile local soil. She may not have hauled her freight very far on that day; but the workaday trips she and all of her sisters later made helped to get the West—and the Western railroads—rolling into an era of enormous growth and prosperity.

Festooned with symbols of earth's bounty and of Mercury, god of travelers, this engine celebrates the rail-farm partnership.

THE STRUGGLE

OF THE

MUSSEL SLOUGH SETTLERS

FOR THEIR HOMES!

AN APPEAL TO THE PEOPLE

HISTORY OF THE LAND TROUBLES IN TU-
LARE AND FRESNO COUNTIES.

THE GRASPING GREED OF THE RAILROAD MONOPOLY.

BY THE SETTLERS' COMMITTEE.

VISALIA:
Delta Printing Establishment,
1880.

A violent clash of stubborn interests

A railroad man turned up at the Henry Brewer homestead at the border of Tulare and Fresno counties, California, on the morning of May 11, 1880. A government man came with him, prepared to evict Brewer from the field of wheat adjoining the homestead. The wheat was prospering because Brewer had devoted five years to cultivating the semi-desert soil of the San Joaquin Valley. But it was growing on railroad land—land granted by the government to the Southern Pacific Railroad along the railroad's right of way—and now the government was about to turn it over to the S.P. to sell to someone else. Curiously, Henry Brewer, who was about to lose both land and crop, stood aloof from the proceedings; he was peacefully plowing another field in a remote corner of his homestead. What Brewer saw from this safe position was a scene of violence and bloodshed that would become known as the Mussel Slough Tragedy.

The government man at Brewer's homestead, a United States marshal named Alonzo Poole, was armed with a pistol and a court order for Brewer's eviction. Accompanying him in a light buggy was the railroad man—a land grader named William Clark, one of the agents who set the prices at which the S.P. proposed to sell its land. Riding separately in a farm wagon were two local customers of Clark's and the railroad's, Mills Hartt and Walter Crow. Earlier that morning, Marshal Poole had evicted a pioneer from another homestead and confirmed Hartt as the new owner of that land. Crow was to receive Brewer's wheat field; he already had paid the railroad $1,624 against a total purchase price of $6,288. Crow and Hartt were armed with three pistols, a Spencer rifle and two shotguns reloaded with big, lethal pistol balls instead of buckshot.

As the buggy and the wagon drove onto the homestead, a party of 15 or more horsemen led by a farmer named James Patterson intercepted them. All or most of these men were armed with pistols, and all had reason to believe they would soon find themselves in Brewer's fix, for since 1878 the railroad had been seeking to evict them from land they had developed to fertility.

Patterson politely informed Marshal Poole that he would not be permitted to serve his eviction papers—but that was the last polite statement made at the confrontation. Suddenly someone demanded that Poole hand over his pistol "on peril of your life." Poole protested that as a United States officer he could not and would not comply, and Patterson agreed to let him keep the weapon but assigned two settlers to guard him. Just then a jostling horse, apparently by accident, knocked Poole down. And a pistol shot crashed out.

The next 30 seconds or so were never fully reconstructed. Almost simultaneously, a farmer named James Harris fell dead with four pistol balls from a shotgun blast in his abdomen, and Hartt fell from the wagon, mortally wounded by a pistol bullet in the belly. Horses panicked and began running in wild circles.

As his team bolted, Crow had seized a shotgun from the wagon, and he apparently did most of the firing that followed. According to some accounts, he brought down a man named Iver Knutson with 12 slugs in the breast. He killed another, Daniel Kelly, shooting him off his runaway horse with a shotgun charge in the back. There was a momentary pause and Crow began to run but, seeing Archibald McGregor trying to dodge behind his horse, he mortally wounded him with two pistol shots, one in the breast, one in the back. Then Crow was challenged by a man named John Hender-

This pamphlet, charging the Southern Pacific Railroad with driving settlers from the Mussel Slough district of the San Joaquin Valley in California, was the prelude to a shoot-out in which seven men were killed.

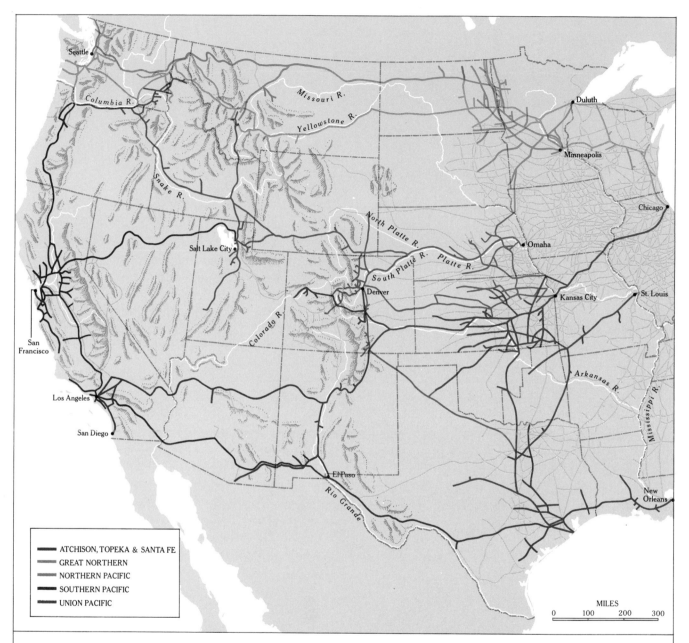

Seattle

Columbia R.

Snake R.

Missouri R.

Yellowstone R.

Duluth

Minneapolis

Chicago

Salt Lake City

North Platte R.

South Platte R. · Platte R.

Omaha

Denver

Kansas City

St. Louis

San Francisco

Colorado R.

Arkansas R.

Mississippi R.

Los Angeles

San Diego

El Paso

Rio Grande

New Orleans

	ATCHISON, TOPEKA & SANTA FE
	GREAT NORTHERN
	NORTHERN PACIFIC
	SOUTHERN PACIFIC
	UNION PACIFIC

MILES
0   100   200   300

THE GREAT RAIL SYSTEMS OF THE WEST

On January 6, 1893, when the last spike of the Great Northern Railway was driven home, the country's sprawling network of transcontinental rail lines was essentially complete. Five long ribbons of track now spanned the West, following the general routes of the first transcontinental rail surveys *(page 21)*.

The five great rail systems (color-coded according to the map legend) were complemented by an intricate web of other main lines, feeders and spurs *(light blue)*. The Union Pacific had flung track north to Washington and south into Texas.

The old Central Pacific had been merged in 1885 with the Southern Pacific, which dominated rail traffic in California and included a transcontinental line east to New Orleans. The Santa Fe owned track from Chicago to Los Angeles, and the Northern Pacific and Great Northern ran from the Great Lakes to the Northwest coast. Altogether, some 40,000 miles of track had been added to the Western railroads in the 1880s alone. Now the building spree was over, and the wail of high-balling locomotives penetrated the farthest reaches of the West.

son, who advanced upon him firing a defective Navy revolver whose cylinder had to be turned by hand between shots. Falling flat each time Henderson raised his clumsy weapon and got off his widely spaced, irregular shots, Crow fired back. He won the exchange, killing Henderson with a bullet in the left breast.

The firing stopped as abruptly as it had begun. A weird, abashed silence fell over the Brewer homestead. Although nearly all the men on the scene had been armed, one man slowly, softly said, "Nobody didn't come here to shoot."

Somebody else said aloud that Crow had fired the first shot, but Crow, raising his pistol again, cried, "I'll be damned if I did." Immediately, Marshal Poole advised Crow to "go to the timber." Crow went first to his dying friend, Hartt, and turned the man over to a more comfortable position. Then, stooping low, he vanished into Brewer's tall wheat. A mile and a half away, on a bridge, somebody whose name was never revealed shot Crow dead with a single bullet in the back.

So seven men fell on a sunny California morning in a battle over the land along one sector of a railroad's right of way. The battle could have erupted along many sections of the right of way of the great land-grant railroads of the West. In this case, the railroad was the Southern Pacific and the battlefield was Mussel Slough.

The violence traced its origin back to 1865, when the S.P. was chartered to build south from San Francisco to Los Angeles and San Diego and received from Congress the customary grants of land along its route. The charter was taken over in 1868 by the Big Four: Leland Stanford, Charles Crocker, Collis Huntington and Mark Hopkins, who had built the Central Pacific. The railroad did not take immediate title to its lands, but it invited settlers to build farms there and declared: "If the settler desires to buy, the Company gives him the first privilege of purchase at the fixed price, which in every case shall only be the value of the land, without regard to improvements. The lands are offered at various figures from $2.50 upwards per acre. Most is for sale at from $2.50 to $5."

Tulare County, in the southern San Joaquin Valley, drew its name from the Spanish word for the rank marsh reeds — *los tulares* — that grew in a section called Mussel Slough, pronounced *sloo* by the people who came there, and named for the fresh-water mussels that

throve among the reeds. In this unappetizing land the settlers staked out fields and set to work.

Many claimed homesteads on land in the public domain, but settlers also staked out farms on the adjoining railroad land, planning to buy them cheap someday. For years it was a threadbare existence. The land was either swampy or desert-like, and in a year of drought it was all desert — "a horrible desert," said one visitor, "with soil generally dry, decomposed and incapable of cultivation," and with "no trace of vegetation but a few straggling artemesias, scorpions and a small but extremely poisonous rattler." By hardscrabble labor the farmers excavated an irrigation system and brought water to the parched soil. By 1878 the land was blooming, rich in barley, wheat and fruit. And the railroad was there, carrying the harvest to market.

In 1878 the railroad took formal title to its land grant and sent men like land grader William Clark to appraise this man-made fertility. These men set the price of the railroad land at $25 to $35 an acre. At first the settlers met the proposition with disbelief, then with outrage. They sent a letter to Charles Crocker to remind him of the railroad's promise of low land prices. He pointed out blandly that the promise had been "$2.50 an acre *upwards*."

The dispute went to the courts. It remained there for years, moving from rung to rung up the ladder of jurisprudence, and the settlers lost every case — in local courts, the U.S. Circuit Court and the United States Supreme Court. Throughout the long litigation, the settlers were never able to conceive that these cases could go against them. In their eyes the justice of their cause was self-evident. They held that the S.P. had forfeited its land grant by failing to follow the original surveyed route. More important, the railroad had broken its promise to the settlers by trying to collect for improvements that they alone had created. Nevertheless, on the final ruling of the courts, more than 200 families were evicted from their homes and lands.

The settlers' case still lay before the Supreme Court on the morning of the killings at the Brewer homestead, and the farmers involved in those killings were popular heroes. That winter, five of these men were found guilty of the minor charge of obstructing a federal officer in the discharge of his duty, and sentenced to six months in jail. Their stay in the Santa Clara County lockup turned

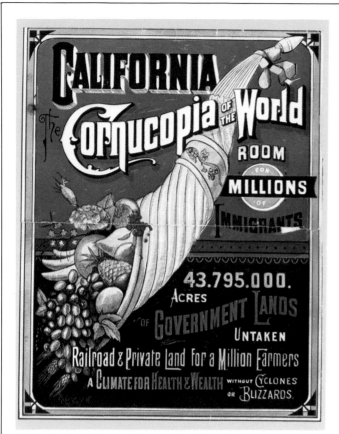

This glowing lithograph is typical of the advertising issued by state immigration bureaus eager to lure tax-paying residents.

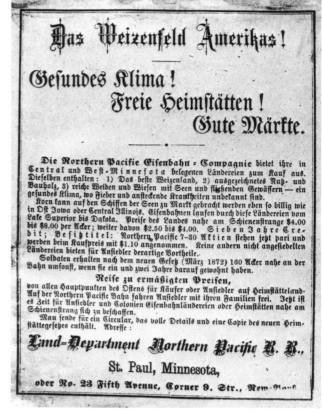

The Northern Pacific in the 1870s plastered Germany with posters extolling cheap wheatland in Minnesota's grand climate.

Dreams nourished by massive propaganda

To attract settlers to fill up the lands abutting their lines, railroads in the West loosed a flood of posters, pamphlets and books extolling the virtues of the rolling prairie. Dissatisfied farmers in the Eastern states were prime targets of this propaganda. But the word was also spread throughout Europe to land-hungry peasants. More than 10 languages, including Welsh, German (*above, right*) and Swedish, carried the pitchmen's spiels. The Santa Fe's daring enlister, C. B. Schmidt, personally lured so many Mennonites out of Russia that he had to dodge czarist authorities, furious at the loss of these excellent farmers.

All of the railroad appeals sang the same siren song: Far from being a fearsome Great American Desert, the Western Plains were a well-watered, fertile Eden yielding 100 bushels of corn or 50 of wheat per acre, plus four-pound potatoes and 20-pound radishes. And the salubrious climate promised to heal all known ills.

Kansas winters were rhapsodized in one brochure as being only two months long; if wood ran out, coal deposits were plentiful; and, anyway, once the Indians had been cleared out and prairie fires ceased, the forests would quickly grow again.

Immigrants were offered reduced ship and land fares. Some railroads provided lodgings for visitors viewing possible sites and sold land for as little as two dollars an acre: 10 per cent down, the rest in easy payments over six or more years.

Western railroads spent fortunes wooing settlers with the lure of dirt-cheap land. For every new resident, whether he bought some of the 116 million acres of Western railroad land or settled on federal land, benefited the roads by generating freight traffic.

Results were overwhelming. More Western acres were settled between 1870 and 1900 than in the previous two and a half centuries. Droughts, depressions, floods, fires, blizzards and grasshoppers drove thousands of the new settlers back to the milder East, but more thousands came and stayed. "We gave [the railroads] an empire composed of an arid desert unfit for the habitation of man," Congressman Charles E. Hooker said in eloquent candor. And the railroads, he added, through their intense promotion, had rewarded the nation with "an empire of hardy and industrious citizens."

Another Northern Pacific ad stressed free land with no mention of the bitter winters of the High Plains.

The Great Northern's short cut to prosperity: Let your hens support you until your orchards mature.

A Santa Fe poster (left) created a lush, subtropical vision across the deserts, mountains and bare plains.

Captured Apache warrior Geronimo (*first row, third from right*) and his band glumly wait out a stop in Texas in 1886. They were being transported east on the Southern Pacific to a detention camp in Florida.

out to be a half-joyous travesty of imprisonment. The doors of their cells were left unlocked; they were permitted to leave the jail now and then; some of their wives and children moved right into the calaboose to serve time with them, and the public saw to it that comfortable family quarters were fitted out and that the larder was always well stocked. Donations of food poured into the jailhouse from the St. James Hotel of San Jose, from Fred Black's chain of California food stores and from individuals in almost every state; a French chef who happened to be serving time in the jailhouse prepared gourmet meals. And the five men ended their imprisonment to public acclaim.

But public opinion alone could not settle the rights and wrongs of the Mussel Slough shoot-out. The Southern Pacific and all the other railroads of the West

had a case of their own — and it was more than a dry and formal legal case. To an extraordinary degree, these railroads claimed and deserved credit for turning the empty West into a cornucopia for man's use.

As early as 1873 author Charles Nordhoff told visitors to the West that "the railroad will seem to you the great fact. Man seems to exist only that the road may be worked." But men had benefited mightily by this "great fact" of the West. The cowboy, for one, was a product of the railroad, for the cattle business depended upon the cattle cars that moved steers to Eastern markets. Lumbermen worked in forests purchased from the railroads, and sent their logs by rail. The fruits of the Northwest and the varied harvests of California became cash crops only when the transcontinental lines began to carry them. Vacation resorts sprouted on rail-

Immigrant Russian families, having ridden west on the Northern Pacific, debark at Bismarck, North Dakota, in the 1880s. More prosperous settlers even brought their own portable houses, trees and shrubbery.

road land, and tourists took the train to get to them.

And to make all these things happen, the railroads literally populated the Old West. Charles Russell Lowell, head of the Burlington & Missouri's land department, saw the railroad's problem early on. In 1859 he said: "We are beginning to find that he who buildeth a railroad west of the Mississippi must also find a population and build up business." James Jerome Hill, the last and possibly the greatest of the railroad empire builders, put the same problem in the form of an epigram: "Population without the prairie is a mob, and the prairie without population is a desert."

So the railroads, to the nation's benefit and their own, filled the lands they crossed. In Kansas alone, between 1870 and 1874, the population leaped upward from 364,000 to 530,000; in 1887 more than a mil-

lion and a half people were living there. By 1880 Western railroads were getting nearly three fourths of their revenue from local traffic — that is, from the people they themselves had placed upon the land.

Now and then, in their urge to populate the wasteland they had bridged, the railroads overdid things a little. From the beginning, for example, railroad promotion set out to erase the popular idea, fostered by Daniel Webster, among others, that the West was the "Great American Desert," fit only for buffalo and Indians. In attacking this concept, the railroads found one friendly ally and one formidable opponent among the men who had conducted the great surveys of the American West.

Their ardent supporter was the scientist and surveyor, Ferdinand Vandiveer Hayden. In his unbridled enthusiasm for the West, Hayden had seized upon the

Locomotives for logging galvanized North-western lumbering in the 1880s, when they replaced ox-drawn wagons to move heavy timber like these logs felled by proud lumberjacks in the forests of Washington.

utterly unscientific idea that "rain follows the plow." According to this optimistic notion, when semiarid lands were plowed the soil would absorb more water; the water would then evaporate and, in proper season, would come back down as rain. The idea fed upon itself to produce still greater wonders: rain would produce crops, and the moist foliage would foster still more evaporation and bigger rains. In time, these rains would even promote the growth of forests. Thus, the Great American Desert would become a man-made paradise.

Railroad land agents all but canonized Hayden and raised his doctrine to the status of holy writ. "The old proverbial drought of the Far West is a thing of history," the Burlington road proclaimed. The Union Pacific declared officially that once the lands around its tracks were settled they would become "one great ab-

sorbent body that might be likened truthfully to a sponge." Hayden himself was both amenable and malleable; a Kansas Pacific land agent reported to his superiors that he had written up "learned reports" on increasing rainfall along the railroad's right of way, and that Hayden had agreed to publish them as his own.

Soon the theory began to expand still further, with friends of the railroads arguing that the lines themselves were rain makers. A Colorado newspaper, for example, proclaimed that the "increase of railroads has the effect of producing more showers. The concussion of air and rapid movement produced by trains and engines affects the electrical conditions of the atmosphere."

Nobody really wanted to scotch Hayden's splendid theory, but John Wesley Powell, one of the great trailblazers of the Old West, felt that he had to. In an ex-

haustive study of land use in the region, Powell had reached the conclusion that much of the West could "maintain but a scanty population." He declared that it was "almost a criminal act to allow thousands to establish homes where they can not maintain themselves." And he argued that the acreage of Western homesteads granted by the government should be raised from 160 to 2,560 acres — that is, from a single quarter-section to four entire sections of land — and that this acreage should be used for pasture rather than crops.

To the railroads and their allies such notions amounted to blasphemy. Powell was excoriated by Martin Maginnis, a territorial delegate to Congress from Montana, as "this revolutionist, this charlatan in science." For a time, in fact, Powell and his ideas were in eclipse; Hayden and his, in the ascendant. During the late 1860s and early 1870s a fortuitous weather cycle seemed to vindicate the optimistic Hayden; annual rainfall increased substantially, and at one point the Santa Fe confidently announced that the rain line along its tracks was advancing at a steady 18 miles per year.

But then, in 1873 and 1874, great droughts occurred, and thousands of farmers failed. Faced with this evidence that providence had no intention of furnishing an Eden in the West, the railroads became a little more realistic. The Union Pacific informed its customers of the necessity of irrigation on the eastern slope of the Rockies, and the Santa Fe warned prospective settlers that "if hard work doesn't agree with you, or you can't get on without luxuries, stay where you are."

At bottom, though, the nature of the propaganda effort did not change. The railroads knew that they had

Tourists bask in the sun against limestone terraces at Wyoming's Yellowstone National Park in 1888. Although the rate was $110 round trip from St. Paul, this group brought a white-aproned servant.

to fill the land with people, and from the first they set out to do so. Almost a year before the Union Pacific drove its golden spike at Promontory, the owners of the line had appointed its chief engineer and onetime surveyor General Grenville Dodge head of the U.P. land department. The office he set up spent over $800,000 advertising Union Pacific land in its first 10 years, some $105,000 in 1874 alone. And as late as 1887, even after those awful droughts, the Rock Island line was blithely assuring anyone who would listen that Kansas was "the garden spot of the world." Why? "Because it will grow anything that any other country will grow and with less work. Because it rains here more than in any other place, and at just the right time."

To carry such messages to the nation, the railroads mounted promotion campaigns of mammoth proportions. The U.P. advertised its lands in 2,311 newspapers and magazines in 1874. Railroads set up promotion booths at expositions at Chicago in '74, Philadelphia in '76 and St. Louis in '78. Maps and guides, some with lavish color illustrations, were distributed by full-time land agents in New York, St. Louis, Atlanta and Washington, D.C. Quarters were provided for emigrants at Omaha and meals were served at a top price of 25 cents. All the literature preached not only the fertility of the plains, but the health, beauty and nobility of people fortunate enough to live in those blessed precincts. Much of it waxed poetic; one brochure spoke of the plow "tickling the Plains and producing in return the laughter of bountiful harvests."

An eloquent fellow named Moses Syndenham made a living by turning out "unsolicited" testimonials, which the railroads distributed by the thousands. Syndenham earned his money partly by fulsome praise of his employers; in one of his poetic flights, he addressed the president of the Burlington & Missouri in these words: "May success attend the energetic efforts of the Burlington, and many benedictions and blessings arise from thousands of homes made happy by the wise dealings and liberal conduct of the company toward those who are homeless and landless in the world."

Now and then, of course, a land agent would go too far. During one period the Astoria & Coast Railroad in the Pacific Northwest had an agent named Paul Schulz who, while the line was still in construction, promoted the sale of its land by promising to name new stations

EDWARD HARRIMAN

THOMAS SCOTT

WILLIAM JACKSON PALMER

DAVID COLTON

JAY GOULD

JOSIAH PERHAM

The financiers: some fortunates, some failures

THOMAS SCOTT worked his way up from station agent to president of the Pennsylvania Railroad, then bought control of so many other lines that he became known as the Pennsylvania Napoleon. In 1871 he was president of five different railroads—including the Union Pacific—a vice president of 12 and a director of 33.

EDWARD HARRIMAN, a Wall Street broker, collected railroads the way other millionaires amassed paintings. After acquiring the U.P. in 1898, he tried to capture every major Western railroad and ended with 75,000 miles of track. Antimonopolist President Teddy Roosevelt called him a "malefactor of great wealth."

WILLIAM JACKSON PALMER, who cut a rail network into the Colorado Rockies without a penny of government aid, was a railroad financier who actually liked trains better than money. He rode in his Denver & Rio Grande engines just for fun. When he sold out for a profit of $1 million, he gave the money to his employees.

DAVID COLTON, financial director of the C.P., pushed hard to become a railroad baron, borrowing heavily to buy C.P. stock. But after his death in 1878, his surviving partners reclaimed the stock, alleging embezzlement. In the eight-year trial that followed, Colton's name was cleared, but his estate was stripped of its assets.

JAY GOULD made his fortune as a director of New York's Erie line by issuing $64 million in fraudulent stock. In 1874 he took his boodle West, bought control of both the U.P. and the Kansas Pacific, sold the K.P. at $10 million profit and used the money to establish a fabulously lucrative rail empire in the Southwest.

JOSIAH PERHAM, who made and lost two fortunes before turning to railroads, got a charter in 1864 to build the Northern Pacific. He tried to raise money with a visionary form of people's capitalism, whereby each of a million Americans would buy a share of stock for $100. But Perham found no takers, and went broke again.

after the buyers. Once, in an ecstasy of salesmanship, he pledged the same station to three different prospects from the town of Yakima. When they discovered his little deception they grew so incensed that Schulz thought it wise to get out of town hidden in a locomotive tender, up to his neck in the water tank.

But the need for new customers continued to grow. At one point the Santa Fe published a solemn scientific forecast that Kansas alone could support a population of 33 million in abundance — and the population of the entire nation that year was 55 million. Therefore, since the United States could not furnish an adequate horde of settlers, the railroads turned to Europe for new blood.

The West needed a hardy farm population willing to undergo privation for the prospect of possessing its own land. With this fact in mind, the railroads and the states they served concentrated their recruiting in northern Europe: Germany, Scandinavia, the Low Countries, England, Wales, Scotland and, most particularly, Russia, where members of the pacifist religious sect of Mennonites were recommended as emigrants by Eugene Schuyler, an American diplomat in St. Petersburg, who described them as "intelligent, industrious, persevering, clean, orderly, moral, temperate and economical."

The Mennonites were willing enough to make the long journey to America but they were also shrewd bargainers. They demanded a guarantee of immunity to military service for at least 50 years and, what was more, freedom from any taxes levied to support any military operation. Kansas and Nebraska obligingly passed laws exempting them from military service; and, in 1873, Secretary of State Hamilton Fish, consulting his crystal ball, offered his absolute personal assurance that the United States "for the next fifty years will not be entangled in another war."

When the first large contingent of Mennonites arrived, Nebraska and the Burlington & Missouri line did their best to swipe them from Kansas and the Santa Fe. Nebraska land agents managed to delay them in Lincoln by mislaying their baggage just long enough to take them on a whirlwind tour of the countryside, during which the railroad men offered the settlers free hay, wells, plank roads and windmills. Despite these temptations, the colony went peaceably on to Kansas.

Prized nearly as highly as the Russian Mennonites were Germans and Scandinavians. To persuade them to emigrate, railroad agents inundated northern Europe with literature, playing heavily on the land hunger of an overcrowded, impoverished peasantry. The emigrants responded by the hundreds of thousands. One Santa Fe agent claimed that he alone fetched 60,000 newcomers to Kansas. As the flood grew, prospective colonists were sometimes treated like merchandise rather than human beings; thus, one agent blandly announced to Governor Samuel Crawford of Kansas, "We can supply several thousand Swedes to be furnished, if ordered now." Only rarely did the agents encounter setbacks, and most of them were minor. One group of Germans, for example, devoted beer drinkers to a man, grumbled that in dry Kansas the prohibition law constituted an "unbearable encroachment on personal liberty."

At first, European governments looked upon the American colonizers with a tolerant eye. But this attitude altered as it became apparent that the U.S. was not merely taking Europe's surplus population, but the most industrious members of that population. Russian officials threw one railroad agent out of the country. England, which had long experience in such matters, set about exporting its paupers and criminals. From 1882 to 1884, a British philanthropic organization spent £69,500 in financing American voyages for destitute orphans; another group persuaded convicts — just before they got out — to accept financial aid and go West. The British stratagem caught on in Sweden, Denmark and Switzerland, and the State Department began to grumble against "positive acts of discourtesy."

But whatever their nature, the emigrants kept coming. Swiftly, the West filled up, and it filled mostly with what one Kansas railroad proudly called "a peaceable, even tempered race, who hate war, love peace, honor their wives, raise honest children, live within their income, and grow rich out of Kansas soil."

For a population so large and so industrious, there had to be towns and cities — and the railroads created them, too, determining their location and importance with a fine, free hand. It became a matter of a railroad's choice whether a town was to become a metropolis, a tank-town whistle stop — or a ghost town. Omaha and Kansas City, for example, grew big largely because railroads chose them as places to jump off across the Missouri River. But hundreds of other small Western towns declined or disappeared entirely because the railroad

Railroad magnate Mark Hopkins' imposing
mansion on San Francisco's Nob Hill was
completed after he died in 1878. The
house was Mrs. Hopkins' pet project but
he dismissed it as the "Hotel de Hopkins."

barons decided to take their lines somewhere else.

When a railroad decided to encourage a town's growth, the town had to deserve the honor and do its bit for the line. To its immediate sorrow—but probably its ultimate good—Denver learned that lesson well. Denver began agitation for the Union Pacific to come through town as soon as Congress passed the Pacific Railroad Act in 1862 and—since it was already a lusty village at the time—confidently expected that the railroad would do so. To facilitate its coming, the municipality dispatched editor William Newton Byers of the *Rocky Mountain News,* who had been a surveyor in his youth, to select a suitable pass for the line to follow through the Rockies. Byers chose Berthoud Pass —which led directly out of Denver.

When Grenville Dodge, acting in his capacity as the U.P.'s chief engineer, chose Evans Pass, more than 100 miles to the northwest, Denver temporarily fell into despair. Cheyenne, a Wyoming outpost through which the main line would pass, was delighted; a Cheyenne newspaper crowed that Dodge's decision had left Denver "too dead to bury." But Denver now began to agitate for a spur line to tie into the U.P.

Somewhat to its surprise, the city found the U.P. willing to help—for a price. The railroad offered to lay the rails, provided Denver would grade the roadbed and subscribe to $500,000 in U.P. bonds. Denver happily put up the money and set to work on the roadbed, using 40,000 ties purchased from the U.P. at a dollar apiece. But that was not the end of Denver's troubles. As the roadbed neared completion, the U.P. met with a new crisis of poverty and declared itself unable to come up with rails or rolling stock unless Denver took another million dollars' worth of bonds. Only after doing so did Denver get its spur line and its trains.

Cheyenne's experience was notably happier. It got its roadbed, rails and rolling stock without paying a penny for them. The U.P. even undertook to lay out the new metropolis, sending General Dodge in person to survey a town plan. In July 1867, the railroad sent in a land agent named R. E. Talpey, who set up shop in a tent and began selling 66-by-132-foot lots at $150 each (before his arrival such lots would have been worthless). Then the U.S. Army announced that it would contribute to Cheyenne by building a substantial installation, Fort Russell, on the outskirts of the

JANE STANFORD
Dumpy and devout, Mrs. Leland Stanford looked like Queen Victoria, and sometimes behaved like her. Widowed in 1893, she used her husband's millions to support Stanford University, which he had founded.

MARY CROCKER
Flamboyantly sociable, Mrs. Charles Crocker made herself San Francisco's première hostess by throwing posh parties at the $2.3 million Crocker mansion on Nob Hill, while smothered in satin, brocade and jewelry.

ARABELLA HUNTINGTON
Mrs. Collis Huntington persuaded her frugal husband to build palatial houses and buy costly art works. Thirteen years after his death she married his nephew, one of the other heirs to the Huntington fortune.

town. Finally, the U.P. ensured Cheyenne's importance by making it a division point and announcing plans for building a roundhouse and machine shops there.

Cheyenne boomed. Within a month Talpey's first customers were reselling their $150 railroad lots for $1,000, and soon thereafter for $2,500. Within three months of the arrival of the rails, Cheyenne had a city government. And when shortly thereafter the people organized Laramie County and attempted to set up territorial government to go with it, they gratefully chose General John Casement, the U.P.'s boss tracklayer, as their first delegate to the U.S. Congress.

Even greater good fortune fell to a Missouri River outpost, alternately called Edwinton and The Crossing, in the Dakota Territory. When the Northern Pacific

tracks arrived there in 1873, the settlement's name was officially changed to Bismarck, after the German statesman Otto von Bismarck. The change of name was strategic: the N.P. was trying to entice German farmers to settle in its territory and to stimulate investments by the German government in its enterprise. Ten years later, the town received a more extraordinary gift from the railroad. At that time the temporary capital of the territory was Yankton, but the permanent location of the capital was in dispute. A commission working largely under the influence of the N.P. was set up to decide the issue, and a champion of the N.P. named Alexander McKenzie, who was then serving as Bismarck's sheriff, undertook to settle the matter.

Under the law, the commission had to meet in Yankton to make its decision, and the people of that place had no intention of letting the decision go the wrong way. They planned to slap an injunction on the commission the moment its members showed their faces in town, and delay the proceedings indefinitely. But the resourceful Mr. McKenzie loaded the commission aboard a special train, provided the members with copious refreshment and ran the train into Yankton in the dead of night. After two minutes within the city limits the train backed out of town and rode off. Soon afterward the commission announced its decision: Bismarck would be the new territorial capital, and it eventually became the capital of the state of North Dakota.

Escapades like these did little harm to the railroads' reputation; if anything, they became subjects of admiring gossip and added to the gaiety of the nation. But in time the first great Western railroads ran out of popularity. The public they created and were designed to serve brought a variety of complaints against them. Taken together, these charges could be lumped under a single term: monopoly. And the worst aspect of the railroads' monopoly was the fact that they had the power to set their own rates—rates that amounted to all the traffic would bear.

Inland shippers found themselves subjected to a particularly detested piece of fiscal sleight of hand called the terminal rate. When a Spokane shipper ordered goods from the East, the Northern Pacific charged him the full freight rate all the way to Puget Sound on the Pacific Coast, some 340 miles away, then charged him again for hauling the merchandise back to its destination. Similarly, a farmer in Corinne, Utah, 25 miles west of Ogden, might order a plow from Chicago. The plow would ride past Corinne on a Southern Pacific train, and the farmer would have to wait until it reached San Francisco and was shipped back to him. He paid full rates both ways—as often as not he also missed a plowing season—and at the end of the transaction he was usually about ready to join such antirailroad groups as the Grangers (page 223).

West of the Sierra, the Southern Pacific held a monopoly over the movement of freight into and out of the San Francisco-Oakland area. At times, the road demanded and shippers helplessly consented to submit their books for railroad inspection. Thereafter rates on such products as ore, fruit or incoming manufactures from the East would be delicately balanced between profit and bankruptcy for the shippers.

Periodically, some malcontent would arise to challenge the S.P.'s control of Western freight and passenger traffic. One such challenger was a seller of coal, salt and books named John L. Davie, a former cowboy and onetime opera singer. In 1894, when Davie applied for a license to build a warehouse on city property on the Oakland waterfront, his permit was delayed by the president of the board of public works—apparently for no better reason than the fact that the Southern Pacific had decided that all warehouses on the Oakland side of San Francisco Bay must be located on railroad land. Frustrated, Davie leased private waterfront footage owned by an oyster company and partly occupied by a gang of squatters known as the Oyster Pirates, one of whom was the budding author Jack London.

Anticipating resistance from the railroad, Davie bought a small arsenal of rifles and ammunition and issued them to the pirates. When Davie ordered some 3,000 tons of coal and let it be known he would take delivery by ship, not rail, he soon found his property being fenced in by railroad employees and his warehouse being demolished. After some preliminary skirmishing, in which a railroad policeman knocked Davie out with a two-by-four, Davie and the pirates counterattacked. With the assistance of an antirailroad mob of local citizens, they routed the railroad's minions and the Oakland police from the scene. Several railroad men were flung into the bay.

In an extension of the conflict, Davie began to run a fast five-cent ferry to compete with the Southern Pacific's older, slower ferries, which held a monopoly over bay traffic and charged 15 cents. In the ensuing jockeying for advantage, Davie had his boat ram and sink an S.P. ferry that was blocking his passage in a narrow estuary. Soon afterward, when the S.P. refused to open a drawbridge to him, he tied a hawser to one of the supporting timbers, then backed away and dumped the bridge into the bay. Davie was arrested for wrecking the bridge, but hostility to the S.P. and its monopoly was so great that a grand jury refused to indict him and he went free to enthusiastic public acclaim.

Just as the railroads were sinking to a low point in public opinion, the last of the great empire builders came

The Wasp, a San Francisco journal, printed this cartoon in May 1881. The states through which the Central Pacific and Southern Pacific ran appear as a patiently suffering ass, whipped by a Chinese coolie and ridden by Huntington, Stanford, and Crocker *(left to right).* The tycoons have the railroad commissioner in a pocket, political institutions tied to the tail of their animal and antirailroad rebels securely caged.

WHEN WILL THIS ASS KICK

upon the scene. In most respects James Jerome Hill followed the pattern of his predecessors. Like them, he had relatively humble beginnings; his first enterprises were a fuel company to supply a Midwestern road with wood and coal and a modest steamship line on the Red River between North Dakota and Minnesota. Then, in 1878, he took control of the financially crippled St. Paul & Pacific line, and from that point on his boundless ambition and enormous talents led him to one achievement after another. Hill built his first long line across the Canadian border to Winnipeg. He crowned that triumph with the completion of the Great Northern in 1893 *(map, page 204)*, and soon afterward he established control over the Northern Pacific. At the midpoint of his career Hill had made himself the undisputed master of a third of all the railroad facilities in the American West. Yet his mastery, by the standards of his day, was benevolent; his despotism was enlightened.

When he built the Great Northern, Hill had to do without the luxuries his predecessors had enjoyed. No grant of land or government loan came his way. So he built without them and, paradoxically, he built better; the rigors of economy denied him the luxury of waste or extravagance. It was no accident that his policies, his personality and the story of his struggles won for him much of the public esteem and approbation his predecessors had squandered.

When he was about 14, playing Indian with his friends in the backwoods of Ontario, a misfired arrow blinded Jim Hill's right eye. It was the only impairment of his faculties he suffered until his last illness, only nine days before his death at 78. Between those events he whetted his enormous energies in contests with most of the railroad and financial colossi of his age. His enemies included Sir William Van Horne, the czar of the Canadian Pacific Railway; Henry Villard, the organizer of the group that for a time controlled the Northern Pacific; Jay Gould, who tried to bluff him out of competing with the Union Pacific; and Edward Henry Harriman, with whom he fought for control of half a dozen railroads. His wars and his competitive instinct won him a dozen nicknames—Little Giant, Oregon Bandit, Empire Builder, Red River Pirate and One-Eyed Old Sonofabitch. When he died, he left $53 million and a superb collection of modern French paintings. Because his wife, a former waitress, was a Roman Catholic, he gave the Church more than a million dollars.

Physically Hill was awesome: short and bandy-legged with a long torso, a huge chest, powerful arms and a thick muscular neck. His spade beard early turned gray, then white, and when he was aroused—which was often—his good eye glared like the headlight of one of his locomotives.

He was capable of outlandish pettiness and equally extravagant generosity. At one time the people of a resort town complained of the noise of his switch engines in the night and the dreary sight of his boxcars and switchmen's privies between the hotel veranda and the lakeshore in daylight. Hill promptly moved the depot two miles out of town. But when he learned that the move had ruined the charter-fishing business of an old friend named Tom Wise, Hill built a fine lakeside pavilion, stocked it with every known brand of fishing tackle, bait and 20 boats and gave it to Wise without charge. When another crony, John Grant, sold his Montana ranch for $20,000 and asked Hill to keep the money for him, he invested the funds in his own ventures; and when Grant at length needed money, Hill gave him back $60,000.

Once, furious at a telephone in his office for no particular reason, he ripped the instrument off the wall and smashed it to smithereens. When a fire broke out in that same office, he saved his records by picking up his 300-pound roll-top desk and heaving it out the window to the street below. On another occasion he asked a new clerk his name; the man replied that he had been christened Charles Swinburne Spittles. "I don't like your name and I don't like your face," Hill snapped, and fired him on the spot.

Despite these private outbursts, Hill brought an enlightened sense of public interest to his empire building, but when the opportunity presented itself, he could be as rapacious as any of his competitors. He built the Great Northern without subsidy because he had to, but in 1891, while it was under construction, he recalled a potentially useful experience out of his past. The Great Northern's parent road was the St. Paul, Minneapolis & Manitoba, which ran from the Twin Cities into the rich Red River valley region of the Dakota Territory. Hill remembered that back in 1857 the government of Minnesota had granted the road 65,000 acres along the Red River. The grant had never been taken up and

the U.S. Land Office, considering it abandoned, had opened the land to homesteading and granted titles to farmers who settled there. But now came Hill, in complete control of the Manitoba line. Appealing to the Supreme Court, he got the old grant reinstated and, with brusque dispatch, began evicting the settlers. In the ensuing uproar, an embarrassed Congress placated Hill by swapping him 65,000 acres of prime timberland in Montana, Idaho and Washington—which was exactly what Hill had had his eye on all along.

But Hill was never a mere absentee manipulator of his railroads. He had a prodigious capacity for detail: a splintered plank in a depot platform, a flatcar that needed repair, a stretch of burned ties where a thoughtless engineer had dumped live coals, a trackwalker whose breath carried a taint of booze. He was a participator. One winter when the Great Northern was snowbound in North Dakota, Hill was there at the face of the drifts. His private car was hitched to the work train, and when he grew impatient with progress through the blocked cuts, he took over a laborer's shovel, sending the man back to warm himself with the empire builder's coffee beside the empire builder's stove.

These were the qualities that Jim Hill brought to the building of his empire, which eventually spread from the Canadian province of Manitoba down to Missouri, from the Great Lakes west to Puget Sound—and on to the Orient by means of his own steamship line. And these qualities were nowhere more evident than in the planning and construction of the Great Northern, the last great Western railroad.

From the first, in the creation of that road, Hill kept two paramount considerations in mind: his engineering had to be superior, because he had no generous Congress behind him; and he had to fill the land with people and profitable employment as he went, for without these his railroad would go broke.

One of his principles was that the G.N. should never tackle a grade that could be avoided. He got through 400 miles of Montana with no grade exceeding 31.7 feet to the mile, and through most of that distance at nothing steeper than 21 feet. To bring the line over the Rockies, he found a 36-year-old engineer named John F. Stevens, who had made an enviable reputation in planning the tortuous route of the Denver & Rio Grande narrow-gauge railroad. Far out in Montana, Hill

Angry farmers taking on the railroads

Many a farmer of the mid-19th Century, attracted by quick profits as well as the prospect of improved access to markets, mortgaged his land for money to buy stock in the building of a nearby railroad. Then, when the line was completed, it too often skinned him coming and going, charging unacceptably high freight rates both for crops shipped and goods bought.

Moreover, as farmers saw it, railroads unfairly gave rebates to big shippers, set higher tariffs on short hauls than they did on long, grabbed much of the West's remaining free land and liberally distributed passes providing free travel to elected representatives who, though sworn to protect the public interest, had voted favorably on the railroads' requests.

The farmers' growing rage, fanned by increasingly hard times, helped Oliver Hudson Kelley in 1867 to launch the National Grange of the Patrons of Husbandry, popularly known as the Grangers. Kelley was a Yankee zealot who toured the nation preaching that all wealth springs from the soil. Within seven years he had organized 1.5 million farmers into 20,000 Grange lodges from coast to coast. Oliver Kelley had conceived the Grangers as a social-cultural order, but farmers assembled at the meetings naturally talked politics, too.

Until the Grangers grew to become a political force, U.S. railroads in the West and other rural areas had behaved pretty much as they pleased. But now, in state after state, new parties reflecting the farmers' grievances began winning elections and passing hastily drawn laws limiting freight and

This lithograph, ennobling the role of farmers, was a standard decoration of most Grange halls.

passenger rates, abolishing passes and creating watchdog commissions.

As times improved, however, farm prices rose and revolutionary ardor cooled. Also, railroad lawyers began to find so many loopholes in "Granger laws" that most were repealed.

Grange meetings then reverted largely to social activities. Nonetheless, the Grangers had inspired laws regulating railroads, and led eventually to the creation of the Interstate Commerce Commission and to a broad consensus that railroads were public utilities.

A large tip from Jim Hill enabled St. Paul waitress Mary Mehegan to enter a Milwaukee school in 1863. Four years later she graduated, made right for St. Paul, married Hill and lived happily ever after.

set Stevens to the job of rediscovering the "lost" Marias River Pass, which Meriwether Lewis had originally learned about from Indians in 1805, but had been unable to locate. Traveling afoot with one Flathead Indian guide (who gave out in the dead of winter), Stevens finally found the gateway in 1889. In time, it lifted the Great Northern over the spine of the country at 5,200 feet on a grade of one per cent.

Hill's second principle called for building an artery of rails that would serve and be served by capillaries all along its length. He called it "protecting the rear." In practice, this meant that every few miles a branch line left the Great Northern's main track to tap some likely source of revenue. Thus, Hill got his tracks into Butte, Montana, to serve a mining colossus that came to be known as Anaconda Copper. Apples were already being grown on a small scale in Washington's Wenatchee valley; remembering a family of Eastern agricultural empire builders on a scale inferior only to his own, he went to Junius Beebe of Boston and persuaded him to plant orchards in Washington. Eventually the Beebe apple ranch needed four and a half miles of G.N. boxcars to ship its yearly crop. Having extracted his 65,000 acres of fir and spruce from Congress, he took a Minnesota friend, the lumber baron Frederick Weyerhaeuser, out there for an inspection trip. The result of the foresighted expedition was the vast timber industry of the Northwest.

Probably more compelling than any of these business opportunities was Hill's interest in the basic American farm. He was a farmer himself; an importer of blooded Polled Angus stock from Scotland, and a man with a fetish for wheat. In his mind's eye Hill saw endless prairies of wheat undulating beyond the horizon on the rising Montana uplands. He was wrong there — it was the only really tragic mistake he made — for the same reason that Ferdinand Vandiveer Hayden had been wrong: rain does *not* follow the plow.

Hill created an agronomy department for the Great Northern, and his experts convinced him that they knew the secret of successful farming on the High Plains.

The recipe called for deep plowing, crop rotation and the practice of leaving fields fallow in alternate summers. It worked at first; and Hill, recruiting in Europe as energetically as any of his rivals, populated a million acres with wheat farmers. But then came a dry cycle and Hill found that he had created a genuine catastrophe: the deep plowing he recommended produced one of the first great dustbowls in the American West.

Except for that disaster, Hill's enlightened self-interest in agriculture paid off handsomely. As a stockman he believed firmly in using the best blood lines obtainable, and before he was through he gave away 7,000 head of purebred breeding stock. Every year he gave farmers three boxcar-loads of high-quality seed grains and they, in their turn, increased the wheat yield along the Great Northern tracks by as much as a third. Because nothing gave him greater distress than the sight of empty rolling stock, he schemed endlessly to keep his boxcars full on their western as well as their eastern runs. To his mind, the Great Northern's terminal on Puget Sound meant more than land's end; to him it was a new commercial horizon. Accordingly he sold rails from Chicago to the Japanese and even persuaded some thousands of rice-loving Chinese to eat wheat flour milled in Minneapolis.

With James Hill the grand era of American railroad building west of the Missouri reached a climax. History would need no more potent testimony than his life and works to the fact that the railroads populated the West, knitted the Atlantic to the Pacific and made the final greatness of America possible. But history often fails to take the measure of a man. It takes other men to do that, and their testimony tends to be cryptic and contradictory. The wheat farmers of Montana spoke of Jim Hill's System; they thought of him as the man who had literally created the world in which they lived. But on their fields those same farmers encountered one particularly persistent, cussed weed that choked their fields and reduced their crop yields. They gave it the half-resentful, half-affectionate name of Jim Hill's mustard.

Oats as tall as a man's eye, harvested on Great Northern land, were shown off in Oregon by farm buff Jim Hill *(left)* and his look-alike son, Louis. Hill even sent a train of agronomists on tour to teach farming.

Chugging forever into the country's culture

Throughout its flamboyant history, the Old West bred heroes whose swashbuckling style became a part of the legendry of the nation. But with the completion of the transcontinental railroad, a new kind of hero captured the country's imagination. Thundering over the rails to Western adventure, the locomotive inspired plays, dime novels and ballads. And standing at center stage with the locomotive were the brave men who guided it through the perils of the High Plains.

This genre of railway drama reached its peak in the 1890s. In 1892 at least a half dozen examples hit the boards. The plots were much alike: most featured bold young trainmen battling red- or white-skinned varmints for the heroine's honor or to protect a trainload of gold. The difference lay in the ingenuity with which the designer of each production fashioned the star attraction—a smoke-snorting dummy engine. *Under the Gaslight* became the first big hit in 1867 because of a locomotive that thundered out of the wings and onto a side track, just missing an actor tied to a main-line track. And in 1899 the acme was reached in *The Fast Mail,* which had two trains chasing each other across the stage.

Railroad fans could also titillate themselves with paperback novels recounting the derring-do of Railroad Rob or Fred Fearnot. And everyone knew at least a chorus from one of the train ballads: those usually mournful plaints about rail workers ("Poor Paddy Works on the Railway") or disasters ("The Wreck of the Old 97") or the railroads' most faithful riders, the hoboes ("The Gila Monster Route").

A holdup gang halts a Western express in this poster advertising an act in Buffalo Bill Cody's tent show. In the show-stopping climax Cody's "Union Pacific Bandit Hunters" galloped in to capture the robbers.

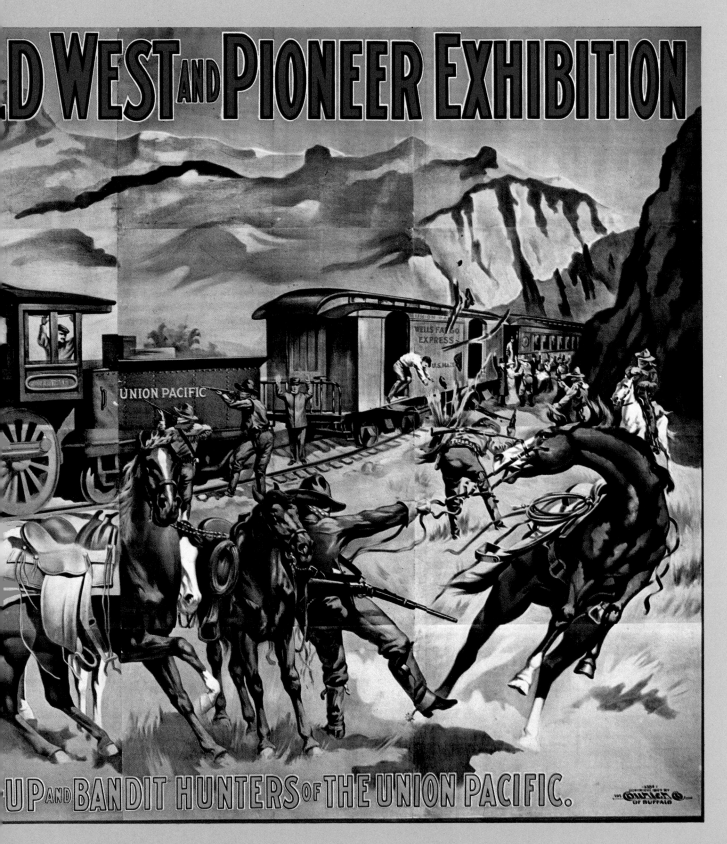

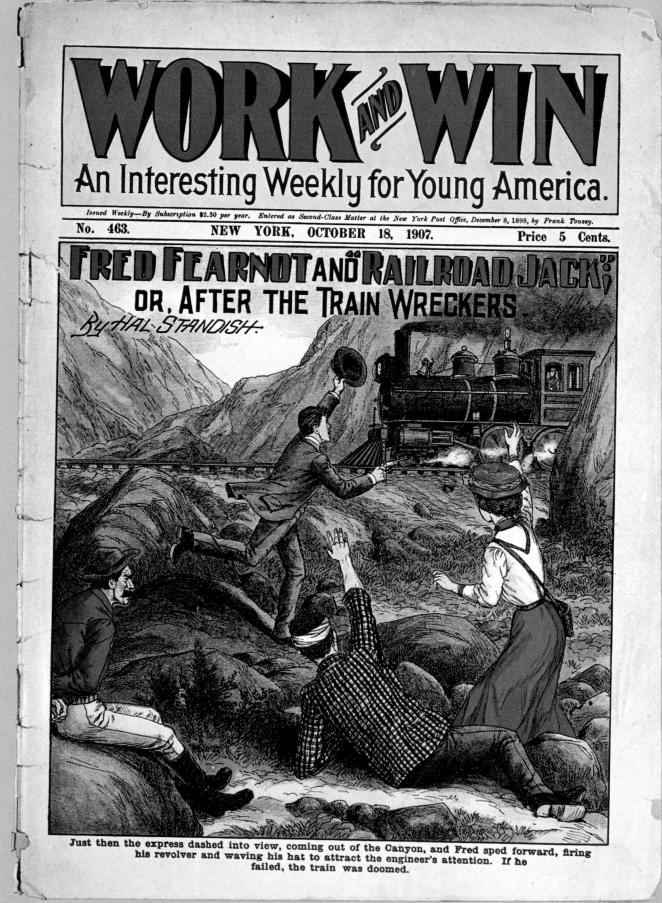

Fred and his girl, having captured the thug *(left)* who had unspiked a track and wounded a section hand *(center),* save a speeding train.

The brave engineer inspired dozens of songs, plays and poems. This march was dedicated to the Brotherhood of Locomotive Engineers.

Oliver Byron played this drama's stationmaster-hero from 1870 to 1900. Its sprawling action moved from slapstick in the Eastern slums

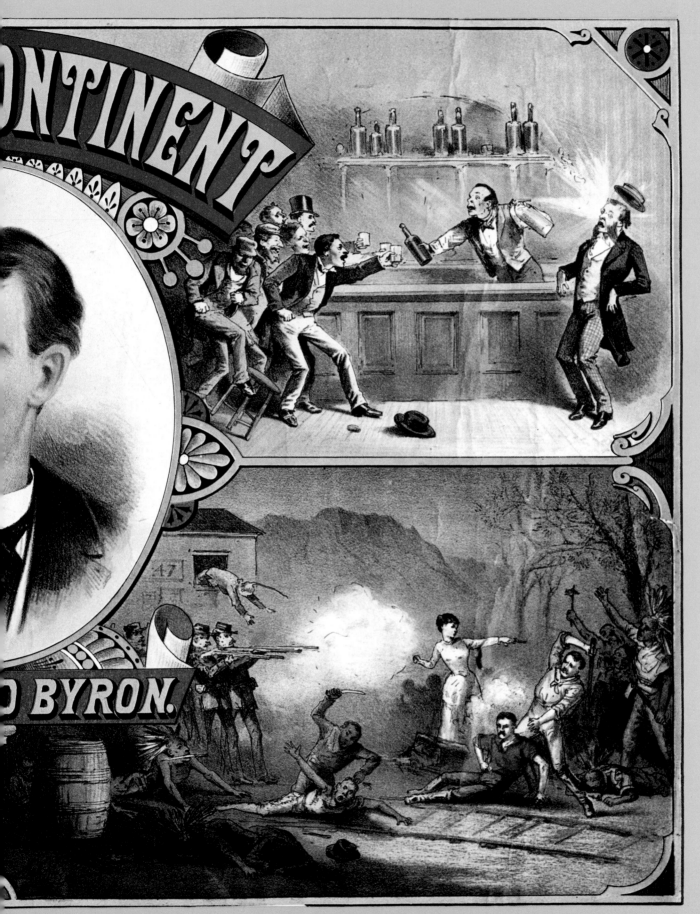

(*top left and right*), to the unmasking of a villain in a rich man's home, to a Western finale where the hero saved his depot from attack.

THE GREAT TR

SENSATIONAL AND STARTLING "HOLD UP" OF TH

In the climax of this 1896 play, a car rolled on stage, dynamite was lit and the sides of the car shattered. One playgoer, the inventor Thomas

Edison, was so impressed that he turned the drama into a motion picture, which, as the first Western, became one of the most famous movies ever.

XXX Printed in U.S.A.